Investigating the Design and Implementation of Operational Safety Plans for Crisis at Higher Education Institutions

Investigating the Design and Implementation of Operational Safety Plans for Crisis at Higher Education Institutions

Antonio Passaro, Jr.

LEXINGTON BOOKS
Lanham • Boulder • New York • London

Published by Lexington Books
An imprint of The Rowman & Littlefield Publishing Group, Inc.
4501 Forbes Boulevard, Suite 200, Lanham, Maryland 20706
www.rowman.com

86-90 Paul Street, London EC2A 4NE

British Library Cataloguing in Publication Information Available

Library of Congress Cataloging-in-Publication Data

ISBN 978-1-66690-352-2 (cloth: alk. paper)
ISBN 978-1-66690-353-9 (electronic)

∞™ The paper used in this publication meets the minimum requirements of American National Standard for Information Sciences—Permanence of Paper for Printed Library Materials, ANSI/NISO Z39.48-1992.

Contents

Foreword

"neVer forgeT" —Virginia Tech "Hokie" Nation
(A first-hand reflection by VT Alumni, Dr. Anne Weiss)

In neuroscience and neuropsychology, how our human brains first create imprints of our lived experiences, and then access those memories across time, is an endless source of fascination. As the seat of knowledge, perception, and personality, our brains process a staggering amount of data at both the conscious and subconscious levels across a lifetime. Most of us will forget the nitty-gritty details of everyday life, including what we ate for breakfast this morning (or, in my case, did I even eat breakfast this morning??? ☺). As we grow older (and, hopefully, wiser), we mentally revisit various events in our lives . . . inevitably accentuating certain details while minimizing others, a tendency that adds plasticity and further subjectivity to the notion of "memory." Thus, as an old adage counsels, there are three sides to every story: yours, mine and the capital 'T'ruth. It is this uniquely human behavior that can leave law enforcement officers and prosecutors highly skeptical of "eye-witness" accounts.

However, due to their inherent affect (a psychological term for the biological experience of feelings or emotions), some events in our life escape this tweaking. If you are a parent, then you probably still vividly remember the day (or night) your daughter or son was born, even if that child is now fully grown with a family of their own. Ask strangers where they were when they heard the news on September 11, 2001, that the Twin Towers had fallen, the Pentagon had been hit, and United Airlines Flight #93 had crashed in Shanksville and they will be able to tell you without hesitation. This phenomenon results from our brain's limbic system, a collection of structures like the hippocampus and amygdala that work together to weave those affective (i.e., emotional) qualities into human memory to create a few relatively stable, long-lasting imprints. The memories below are offered as illustrations of 1) the biological tendency of crisis survivors to never quite forget the trauma of "that day," and 2) the imperative for administrators and emergency management to design effective operational safety plans that can mitigate, to the extent possible, lasting psychological, organizational, and financial impacts from crises.

Tuesday, September 17, 1996, began as a very ordinary day in "Happy Valley" (State College, PA). At twenty-two years young, I was a fifth-year senior ("super" senior as we were called), focused on typical Penn State Nittany Lion student concerns: the first round of exams and projects that come due during Week #4 of a fall semester, could JoePa (Joe Paterno) and his team run through the Big Ten football schedule after a 3–0 non-conference start, and (most important) which flavors of Creamery ice cream would be on the dinner menu that night in the dining commons. My father had just celebrated his sixtieth birthday the day before so my sister, Leigh (a junior at Vanderbilt University in Nashville, TN), I and other family members across the country had jammed up phone lines at the house in Wausau, WI, where he, my mom and my other sister, Debra, lived. Although Dad and I were not exactly on the best of terms back then (I had transferred from his beloved alma mater, the University of Wisconsin-Madison, two years prior under unhappy circumstances), my birthday call to him on September 16 had been amiable and congenial, albeit superficial. In other words, routine.

When I woke up that gray Tuesday morning in 414 Leete Hall, the primary things on my radar were: 1) the day's HIST 427 (German History since 1860) and BMB 401 (Biochemistry I) class meetings, 2) an afternoon "date" (i.e., workout) with a Concept II ergometer (rowing machine) in the Natatorium Loft, 3) my Head of the Cuyahoga River regatta/rowing race that coming Saturday (September 21, 1996) in Cleveland, OH, and 4) my boyfriend, Christopher, and his father, David, traveling to Salt Lake City, UT, for medical reasons. After donning some suitable workout clothes, I grabbed my bookbag and headed south. Although Professor Silverman's HIST 427 class was in the ubiquitous Willard Building (every Penn Stater has at LEAST one class in there during the four or five years we are on campus), I had just enough time before the 9:45 a.m. lecture to swing by the Hetzel Union Building (HUB) to grab a breakfast sandwich from the appropriately named "Fast Break" snack bar. Upon receiving my to-go bag from the cashier, as I had so many other mornings during my 2.5 years on the University Park main campus, I exited the HUB on its south side, which faced the expansive lawn with its rolling hill that terminated at College Avenue. I then joined several hundred students (and a few opportunistic squirrels hoping for dropped breakfast food) negotiating the class transition period along the sidewalk that ran between the HUB building and the lawn's northern grassy edge.

We had no idea that, at the same time, Jillian Robbins was laying a tarp down under the trees and large shrubbery that obscured the HUB Lawn's northwest corner (mere feet from the sidewalk where we were walking). We had no idea that she had with her a 7-mm Mauser (high-powered) military rifle and ammunition. And we had no idea that the tranquility of our safe haven, nestled in the gentle mountains of central Pennsylvania, was minutes away from being shattered by an attempted mass shooting. Many of us in that HUB Lawn crowd, including myself, made it safely to our classes and dorms before the bullets started flying. Melanie Spalla and Nicholas Mensah were not as lucky. Melanie, a junior, died at the scene while Nicholas, a senior, was critically injured from a shot to his abdomen. He would survive. The casualty count would have been higher had it not been for Brendon Malovrh, who found Robbins and wrestled the Mauser rifle away from her before she then attempted to stab him.

Pandemonium and the media descended on State College. In the fall of 1996, Paducah (1997), Jonesboro (1998), Columbine (1999), Virginia Tech (2007), Northern Illinois (2008), Sandy Hook (2012), and so many others were not yet known. Our new president, Dr. Graham B. Spanier, had only just completed his first full year at the helm, having recently arrived from the University of Nebraska-Lincoln, which itself had experienced an almost mass shooting a few years before Spanier left for Penn State. There was no operational safety plan. There was no communications plan, just hastily arranged press conferences for which public relations officers were literally running handwritten notes back and forth between Old Main (which housed Penn State's senior leadership offices) and the HUB. There were no cell phones, no text messages. We students were told to get to a phone as soon as we could to call our loved ones to let them know we were alright because the emergency hotline that the University had set up was instantly overwhelmed. I went back to the HUB and stood in one of several lengthy lines to use the handful of phone booths (yes, phone booths!!) that were in the building back then.

My father was grumpy and gruff when he picked up, and utterly confused when he realized it was me calling so soon after our conversation the previous evening. He had not yet seen any of the CNN coverage so, in those precious few moments allotted to me in that HUB phone booth that morning, Dad never completely understood why I kept repeating I was safe and that I loved him and Mom in a shaky voice that kept breaking as I struggled to articulate what had happened and just how close I had been to it. It was not until later, when Mom came home from work and they saw the images on the

CBS Evening News, that it hit them. Joint phone calls from my parents rarely happened (they either took turns or just one of them, usually Mom, would be on the phone); that night, both Mom and Dad were on the line when they called to check on me.

We spent the rest of the day in bewildered shock. After talking to Dad, I went back to my dorm room in Leete Hall to find that Christopher and David HAD seen the CNN coverage as evidenced by the multiple messages on my answering machine from them. Christopher, a recent Spring 1996 Penn State graduate, had personally brought me back to campus for the Fall semester so he could spend time with me and the remainder of our floor friends who had not yet graduated. He stayed the first three weeks of the semester; he left State College to go back west just the previous week. As a result, Christopher knew my class schedule very well and, knowing my breakfast habits, he suspected that there was an extremely high probability that I had been in the area at the time of the shooting. Because they were traveling, I could not call them back, but rather I had to wait until they stopped along the road and tried me again. Words do not adequately capture their joint relief at hearing my voice before Christopher queried, "what the hell is going on over there?" As I had with my own father, I did my best to relate to them what little we knew at that point in those first few hours (more rumor than fact unfortunately), but I was emotionally spent, confused, scared, and bereaved. I did not personally know the victims, but the Penn State community (like many college campuses) is a close-knit one. This hurt . . . A LOT.

Nearly eleven years later, some of the first students I had the privilege of teaching physical sciences to at Colonial Beach (VA) High School were completing their sophomore year of college at Virginia Tech University. Thanks to Facebook, I have reconnected with several of them over the years. This is what one of them posted on April 16, 2013:

> 6 years ago today, I sat huddled with my roommates watching the news. I remember how scared I was not knowing where all of my friends were, or if they were safe. I remember being so thankful when they started calling, emailing, and showing up to our town house to let us know they were okay and to see how we were doing. I remember being grateful that I could call home and let everyone in my small community know that its Hokies were all okay. I remember feeling guilty that not everyone would get to make that same call. And I remember my first time back on campus after it happened. I remember the woman from a local church who came up to me, handed me some homemade cookies, gave me a hug and told me that I was loved and that everything would be okay. And I remember, in that moment, that I was never more proud

to be part of a community that showed such strength and compassion in our time of need. neVer forgeT

I read my student's words, and many different emotions hit me like a ton of bricks. It was like being taken back in time; I knew exactly how she and her fellow Hokies had felt on that awful spring day in 2007. Approximately 370 miles to the north, I was returning from a harrowing personal ordeal at the Bellefonte (PA) courthouse with my beloved cat, Penny, when I heard the news on the taxi's radio. Blacksburg, VA, is not all that different from State College, PA: rural, nestled in the Appalachian mountains, close-knit, and fiercely devoted to the land grant university at the heart of its community. Many students, particularly engineering majors, attend both schools in some combination, creating to a unique kinship between the two higher education institutions. Tragically, one of our own, Jeremy Herbstritt ('03, '06 PSU Engineering), a graduate student, was among the thirty-two VT victims.

Nittany Nation was galvanized, despite the fact that many of our undergraduates had only been young children back in 1996 and, therefore, had little to no personal experience with Penn State's shooting incident. Student groups coordinated with McLanahan's and the Student Book Store (SBS) down on College Avenue to provide locations where we could sign cards and banners in support and solidarity with Hokie Nation. Within days, it was decided that shirts in maroon and orange would be sold to raise funds for all thirty-two of the victims' families. Initial estimates were that a few hundred would sell; McLanahan's and SBS struggled to keep up with the spectacular demand. It took a couple of days before I finally secured my own shirt.

Given the time of year, football programs all across the country were deep into the NCAA's prescribed two weeks of official spring practices. Many programs hold an annual scrimmage game at its conclusion, which in many places becomes almost as large as a home game event with thousands of alumni returning to tailgate and preview the coming season's squad. Our Blue-White game is no exception; Beaver Stadium/State College becomes like the fourth largest city in Pennsylvania during any home football contest. In response to what had happened at Virginia Tech, there was unanimous consensus at Penn State that our Blue-White game, scheduled for April 21, 2007, would become the Maroon-Orange game. When Coach Joe Paterno held his customary press conference that morning, he carried in one of Jeremy's VT baseball caps that the Herbstritt family had given him and held it in his hands as he took reporters' questions. One of our stadium traditions, Card Block, in which a student section holds up pieces of cardboard to spell out various cheers in blue and white, was quickly re-configured so we could form the "VT" logo in maroon and orange. Much like a White-Out, the call was put out to wear something maroon, orange or both to show our support during our scrimmage. It had been expected that it would be the students who would primarily be the ones in VT colors while the rest of the stadium would be in blue and white, mostly because alumni might not have had the time or interest in tracking down maroon and orange apparel on such short notice. But alumni came through in a BIG way. It is nearly impossible to describe how surreal those few days were, seeing maroon and orange everywhere in a blue and white town, but Hokie Nation deeply appreciated all that we did to support them in their time of bereavement. There are few times when I have been prouder to be a Nittany Lion than then.

Although the Virginia Tech report (and others like it) shone a spotlight on the lapses in emergency management that compounded the impacts of that crisis, I never really questioned whether or not universities would learn the lessons and apply them in enhancing future responses (i.e., their operational safety plans). The ensuing pain and anguish of not only the victims, but also the resulting panic and anxiety of the larger campus community kind of made the concept a no-brainer: who doesn't want to take any and all steps available to improve a response to crisis?

As luck would have it, Special Agent Antonio Passaro, Jr., originally wanted to research active shooter events. In one of his doctoral seminars, Antonio examined if there might be particular variables that could predict such events on a college campus. The project required that he first compile a database of all campus shootings. The September 17, 1996, Penn State shooting was in it. At the time, I remember making a few comments and showing him the Daily Collegian picture above of me in the phone booth calling my dad. I think that Antonio was perceptive enough to recognize that that shooting had left an indelible imprint on me. But I do not sense that he has ever realized the full psychological impact of that memory all these years later. This will be the first time that he, along with you the reader, hears directly from the frightened twenty-two-year-old me, struggling to comprehend what has just happened on my campus.

As professor and law enforcement officer, sworn to protect people like me, Dr. Passaro has a perspective that makes him uniquely qualified to discuss the topics presented here. Thus, when he asked me to look over an early version of his dissertation, I agreed . . . in part because I was curious to learn what progress had been made in research-based design and implementation of operational safety plans that would keep other students from experiencing what I had gone through on September 17, 1996. I was more than a little shocked to discover that, for all the media attention and human suffering, the field still lacks relatively few accepted "best practices."

It is my personal belief that the voices and experiences of survivors, regardless of whether we were hit by a bullet or not, are equally important for putting human faces and raw emotions to what all too easily could become a sterile academic exercise. It has not been easy to write down my experiences (although it has been cathartic) nor will it have been easy for you the reader to read. But Melanie, Jeremy, and so many others who were taken far too soon from a college campus can no longer raise their voices in advocating for progress. I sincerely hope that Dr. Passaro's book succeeds in making a difference as a catalyst for some much-needed action on the critical issue of adequately preparing for future crises.

Anne E. Weiss, Ph.D.
Penn State University Alumna
Classes of 1998 and 2017

Prologue

It is evident that organizations have and will deal with crisis situations at some point during their existence. Unfortunately, higher education institution administrators' focus is on crisis and its aftermath, not necessarily the factors or events that lead to it (i.e., "incubation period") (Roux-Dufort, 2007, p. 106; Sutcliffe, 2018). There are two ways to approach a crisis, which is either an "event-centered approach" or "processual approach" (Roux-Dufort, 2007, p. 108). The premise behind the "event-centered approach" (Roux-Dufort, 2007, p. 108) is the perspective of looking at the event in and of itself as THE crisis, but in reality, it is the damage that threatens life, property, environment, and/or critical systems caused by the event that is the TRUE crisis (EMAP, 2016, p. 1). To illustrate, a tornado can touch down in a location, causing no damage, but a quarter mile away it can wipe out an entire community (Seltzer, 2018). Under this approach, emergency managers, college administrators, first responders, etc. take a reactive approach in dealing with the crisis' aftermath. For example, an EF-4 tornado touched down in Tuscaloosa, causing the loss of fifty-two people, which included six University of Alabama students and one employee, and power as well as damaging or destroying buildings in the area. During this event, school officials communicated using a variety of social networks, PA systems, and media outlets as well as canceling classes, and activating the University's command center to further update and coordinate responses as the tornado unfolded (Nelson, 2014).

Researchers have and are currently exploring the utility of a processual approach as part of the development of a crisis management theory, which could aid in preparing for major catastrophes (Roux-Dufort, 2007). The processual approach is a perception that a crisis is a triggering event that happens after a sequence of events that occurs during the incubation period (Roux-Dufort, 2007). It is looking at the same problem in a different way. One way is not necessarily wrong, it is just different from the other. This is best illustrated by the cartoon on the following page.

Figure P.1.   Hutchison (2015)

So instead of looking at a crisis as event-centered, researchers suggest that crisis managers look at disasters from a different angle (Roux-Dufort, 2007; Sutcliffe, 2018). Researchers suggest that taking this different viewpoint will help to understand (i.e., the incubation period) and to better prepare for catastrophic events regardless of whether it is a manmade or natural event (Roux-Dufort, 2007; Booker, 2014). Under this processual approach, supporters posit that there are components which combine and contribute to trigger THE crisis, regardless of whether it is a manmade, natural, or technological event (Booker, 2014; Denham & Khemka, 2018; Roux-Dufort, 2007; Sutcliffe, 2018).

Combining the event-centered approach with the processual approach can help to define crisis or critical incident. The research literature on crisis management has been primarily focused on the event-centered approach. According to Sutcliffe (2018), "research has largely focused on crises that are large and highly visible (e.g., high consequence, low probability events) and has focused mostly on crisis management after the fact" (p. 486). She further stated that "scholars have neglected incubating processes and other dynamics that precede or may lead to crises" (Sutcliffe, 2018, p. 486). Thus, defining crisis or critical incident reflects the heavy influence of this event-centered approach. Therefore, a crisis or critical incident is a "natural disaster, technological failure, or other emergency that seriously degrades or threatens the safety and security of an individual, a community, or the nation. . . . deployment of resources to manage [locally] an immediate threat requiring multi-disciplinary emergency-services response" (Johns & Jarvis, 2016, p. 1). Furthermore, federal and state agencies use crisis, critical incident, disaster, and emergency interchangeably. To illustrate, EMAP (2016) defines Disaster as, "A severe or prolonged emergency that threatens life, property, environment and/or critical systems" (p. 1), while FEMA (2012) classifies Emergency as,

"Any occurrence, or threat thereof, whether natural or caused by man, in war or in peace, which results or may result in substantial injury or harm to the population, substantial damage to or loss of property, or substantial harm to the environment and is beyond the capacity of an individual jurisdiction to effectively control" (p. 83). In combining event-centered and processual approaches in understanding crises, the argument put forth in this book is that organizations are better equipped to design and implement operational safety plans that more effectively manage risk and bolster resiliency when they focus on the "incubation" period (i.e., the proactive planning and resources needed ahead of the event) rather than reacting as the crisis unfolds in real time (Boin, Hart, Stern, & Sundelius, 2005; Sutcliffe, 2018; van der Vegt, Essens, Wahlstrom, & George, 2015).

The calling, the vision, the reality: As a young child, I had a vision (i.e., a calling) to be a police officer after watching neighborhood kids get into minor trouble and seeing local police officers respond to it. Although I would briefly consider other professions, the tug of law enforcement became inescapable, eventually pulling me into an associate's degree program at the local community college before an unheard-of recruitment into the Virginia State Police Academy at age twenty-two. To this day, I still can vividly remember raising my hand, with my proud parents and family looking on from the stands, as I recited the following Trooper's Pledge with my class on Graduation Day:

> . . . to perform my duties honestly and faithfully to the best of my ability and without fear, favor or prejudice. I shall aid those in danger or distress, and shall strive always to make my State and Country a safer place in which to live. I shall wage unceasing war against crime in all its forms, and shall consider no sacrifice too great in the performance of my duty. I shall obey the laws of the United States of America and of the Commonwealth of Virginia, and shall support and defend their constitutions against all enemies whomsoever, foreign and domestic . . . —Virginia State Police

They say that a dream and its reality can be two very different things. There were many ups and downs throughout my law enforcement officer career: days that I never want to forget and others I want more than anything to forget. One of those days involved traffic control duty in Isle of Wight County for one of the thirty-two victims of the April 16, 2007, massacre at Virginia Tech University. I did not know her personally, but as a parent I could not stop thinking about the victim's parents who must have so proudly seen their daughter off to college (perhaps even driving her up to Blacksburg, VA, themselves and helping her move in), only to now be burying their child under the most heart-rending circumstances. As I stoically motioned the cars into the church's parking lot and then back out after the funeral, my mind wandered to how this scene must be repeating itself in thirty-one other locations, thirty-one other families that would never be whole because a child or a parent was never coming home. And I wondered, with silent rage, there must be something that could be done to prevent another gunman from wreaking such unspeakable suffering on other innocent families.

Because of my sworn duty to care (i.e., to go beyond the call of duty) as well as my subsequent service as criminal justice professor and department chair at my alma mater, I have sought out challenges and pathways that could offer ways for me to serve that might not necessarily have been available to me had I remained solely with the State Police. This passion was stoked further by an almost active shooter situation where I worked several years back. A student walked into a women's restroom and held a female professor at gunpoint. Fortunately, the professor was able to get away, no shots were fired, and the perpetrator was quickly apprehended. However, the incident revealed disturbing deficiencies in the college's operational safety plan when it came to communication with campus stakeholders, lack of training among those administrators who were primarily responsible for executing the college's early response to the incident, and breakdown of relationships between the college, the hired security company and the local police department. We were lucky that the incident was not more serious than it actually turned out.

Both of these experiences, among others, provide the foundation for this book. As I progressed through my doctoral studies, I brainstormed dissertation ideas, and what eventually coalesced in my mind was an examination of operational safety plans for colleges, universities, and affiliated institutions (e.g., K–12, churches, businesses, etc.). While much research has been devoted to understanding why gunmen like the Virginia Tech shooter pull the trigger or why natural disasters are increasing in their destructive intensity, I felt that there was a lack of studies addressing effective design and implementation of operational safety plans, a set of "best practices," if you will, that exists in other fields. I created and executed many operational safety plans as a law enforcement officer; certainly, I could bring my professional experience and expertise to bear on this challenge. And, in doing so, I could continue the tradition that I exercised every day as I got behind the wheel of my police vehicle: I would recite the oath I pledged so many years ago on my Graduation Day from the Academy that compels me to " . . . *strive always to make my State and Country a safer place in which to live . . .*" I hope that, when reading this book, the work resonates with you and finds a place in your organization's operational safety planning protocols because, after all:

Salus populi suprema lex.

The safety of the people is the highest law. —Cicero

Acknowledgments

Whom to acknowledge? This should be straightforward to answer; however, it's complicated because we all are evolving every day, and the answer can change instantly. People can come into your life (short- and long-term), sometimes unexpectedly.

> In life, you will meet two types of people: The ones who will build you up, and the ones who will tear you down. But in the end, you will thank them both.
> —Joseph Esber

Allow me to first take this space to thank the many special people who have contributed to the successful completion of this dissertation journey. I extend my deepest appreciation to my committee members for their patience and hours of guidance during my research and then editing of this manuscript. The untiring efforts of my major advisor deserve special recognition and so I want to thank you, Dr. Dennis Gregory, for *everything!* You have always had my best interests at heart, from the moment I introduced myself to you in your office to our very first class together, *Law in Higher Education*, to degree completion. To Dr. Mitchell Williams, thank you for your guidance as well as sharing your roadmap to a successful dissertation. I'll never forget the key component to any writing (as you always admonished): "Be parsimonious!" To Dr. David Earnest, I am forever indebted to you for placing me on this path in Higher Education Leadership. From the moment we met, you had the utmost confidence in my abilities and you always did everything to express that to me through your advice and uplifting words of encouragement. Thus, I must say I had the *best* committee that any doctoral candidate could ask for; individuals who have *helped* me to fill voids in my life. I also want to thank my family and friends for their patience and understanding while I went through this rigorous, arduous process. I know that it was not easy for you either . . . so a *special thanks* to you all as well. Lastly, I want to say thank you again to a few friends and colleagues that contributed to the review and revision of this book, Dr. Anne E. Weiss, Amy R. Moler, Carol Gillespie, and William Whitley Pearsall, J.D.

I would like to take the remaining space to share some enlightening thoughts I had as I wrote these acknowledgments. In many respects, I had never planned to be in this position, but people came into my life who disrupted the path I was traversing and I was forced to view my world through a new and unfamiliar lens. People come and go from our lives (i.e., what I like to call having a shelf life) for a reason and usually it isn't until after they are long gone that we realize their impact on our lives. However, a handful of corrupt and arrogant law enforcement supervisors immediately through their actions became my greatest motivator. Their behavior reminds me that:

Power corrupts, and absolute power corrupts absolutely. —Lord Acton

If they had not conspired to tear me and my colleagues down, I might not be where I am today and the person I am now. I have been told that it is okay to let people in, and to start over. Behavior and attitudes are developed over a lifetime ("*they*" will never change). I have learned to be mentally strong, and to keep moving and falling forward. The past should not define you, but it should be used as an opportunity to grow and do better in the future. You create your own reality. It's not *what* happens to you in life; it is *how* you respond to it and it starts in the mind. Your thoughts generate your feelings, which drive your behavior, which in turn create your reality so focus on what you can control not what you cannot. While I thank the generous, kind and wonderful people who stood by me as I picked up the pieces, I must also thank those corrupt individuals who attempted to tear me down . . . freeing me to build something better than what they tried to destroy. All that matters is respect, integrity, loyalty, valor, and hope.

Introduction

Imagine that a parent accesses their favorite news network as he or she sits down with a cup of coffee, and there they find live coverage of a mass shooting incident unfolding at the college their child is attending. Alternatively, a parent learns from an emergency text alert that their child's university is on lockdown status (i.e., shelter in place) stemming from a hostage situation about which few details are known. Finally, picture two retired parents setting off for a vacation in the Bahamas only to learn, from social media after checking in, that a massive tornado has ripped through their child's college. These scenarios can (and have) also occur(red) at K–12 schools, shopping centers or malls, businesses and churches; high-profile natural and manmade incidents at college-affiliated institutions have garnered increasing attention from both media and academia (Fox & Levin, 2015).

Although American colleges and universities are no longer bound by the legal doctrine *in loco parentis*, these institutions still have a "duty of care" (Lee, 2011, p. 77) to their students as well as an obligation to provide a reasonably secure work environment to university employees (i.e., faculty and staff) (Griffin, 2009). Given the unexpected nature of natural or manmade disasters, it can be very challenging to maintain these standards (Lee, 2011). For example, 2005's Category 5 Hurricane Katrina swept through the Gulf of Mexico, leaving a trail of destruction from central Florida to eastern Texas with New Orleans taking the brunt of the damage (U.S. Department of Homeland Security, 2006; van Heerden & Bryan, 2006). Three historically black colleges and universities (HBCUs) suffered significant adverse economic impacts from physical flooding, which damaged buildings and destroyed students' records, and students having to attend other institutions during the remainder of the fall 2005 semester (van Heerden & Bryan, 2006; Johnson & Rainey, 2007). An additional example would be the 2007 tragic massacre at Virginia Tech, where the shooter took thirty-two lives before turning his gun on himself (Virginia Tech Review Panel, 2007). Mass confusion dominated because emergency personnel were at a disadvantage from a lack of communication and miscommunication. The handling of this mass shooting eventually triggered civil lawsuits and financial settlements against the University (Lipka, 2007; Lipka, 2008).

Given that disasters like the aforementioned examples can change lives in an instant, operational safety plans guide stakeholders through unforeseen calamitous incidents with instructions answering the "who, what, when, where, and how" details of their responses (Griffin, 2009; Oliver, 2009; Waugh, 2004). College-affiliated institutions create their own unique emergency plans in order to mitigate tort liability and satisfy governmental regulations with the objective of deterring, reducing, controlling, and minimizing damages caused by these unfortunate events (Fox & Savage, 2009; Mumper, Gladieux, King, & Corrigan, 2016; Randazzo & Plummer, 2009). The 2007 Virginia Tech massacre served as the catalyst for change, enhancements, and the formalization of educational institutions' operational safety plans, which were haphazard prior to this event, for manmade or natural disasters (Asmussen & Creswell, 2013; Randazzo & Plummer, 2009; Virginia Tech Review Panel, 2007). In fact, some states, such as Virginia, mandated the creation of Care and Threat Assessment Teams (legislative Code of Virginia 23-9.2:10 [effective March 7, 2008] and 23.1-805 [effective October 1, 2016]) for all higher education institutions as well as violence prevention committees. Although the overall goal of campus emergency planners is to keep people safe, little is known in the literature about what constitutes the essential components necessary for efficacious operational safety plans (Thompson, Price, Mrdjenovich, & Khubchandani, 2009). Furthermore, there is anecdotal evidence to suggest that these plans have deficiencies, which do not become apparent until the plan is utilized during an actual crisis. Thus, this research will explore "best practices" for design and implementation of operational safety plans, which can potentially inform future enhancements.

BACKGROUND OF EMERGENCY MANAGEMENT

Historically, colleges and universities have always faced challenges with keeping their employees and students safe. The uncertainty or rather the unpredictability of natural and manmade disasters is the primary issue with which institutions have to cope. Natural disasters, such as hurricanes, tornadoes, forest fires, snowstorms, and earthquakes, will occur eventually for a particular area, but it is unclear ahead of time when, where, and how intense those events will be. For example, meteorologists predict hurricanes mainly through computer models that approximate a certain time for landfall (URI, 2015). The prediction of Hurricane Florence in summer 2018 forced governmental officials to issue an emergency evacuation alert to the residents of North Carolina, South Carolina, and Virginia (Rodgers, 2018). Administrators of Virginia colleges and universities suspended their operations and advised faculty and students to take necessary precautions. However, the hurricane unexpectedly shifted south, which spared Virginia the most serious effects of a direct hit. For Virginia, these emergency preparations cost institutions financial resources and lost instructional time (Albiges, 2018).

Manmade disasters such as active shooter situations, bomb threats, and other violent crimes that grab the media's attention, are unpredictable or met with a great deal of incredulity prior to their occurrence even with tips or advanced intelligence to law enforcement (National Commission on Terrorist Attacks upon the United States, 2004). To illustrate the difficulty with which most people can envision catastrophes before they happen, no one could have imagined using passenger aircraft as weapons prior to September 11, 2001 (National Commission on Terrorist Attacks upon the United States, 2004). Another example would be what is considered the 9/11 of mass shootings: the 2007 Virginia Tech massacre (Virginia Tech Review Panel, 2007). Even though there were isolated patterns of behavior that caused particular individuals concern, how those puzzle pieces fit together only became tragically clear after the shooting or planes striking the Twin Towers. Søren Kierkegaard said it best when he said, "Life can only be understood backward; but it must be lived forward" (Kierkegaard, 1843).

Higher education institutions, for much of their histories, had emergency preparedness plans that were nonexistent or limited in scope. On October 12, 1992, a student, Arthur McElroy, at the University of Nebraska-Lincoln (UNL), attempted to shoot his peers when his rifle jammed upon pulling the trigger. This could have resulted in one of the first mass casualty events on a college campus. Asmussen and Creswell (2013) discovered that:

> [UNL's] lack of a formal plan to deal with such gun incidents was surprising, given the existence of formal written plans on campus that addressed various other emergencies: bomb threats, chemical spills, fires, earthquakes, explosions, electrical storms, radiation accidents, tornadoes, hazardous material spills, snowstorms, and numerous medical emergencies. (p. 410)

Natural disasters that do not normally strike particular regions pose unique challenges for the nation's colleges and universities. For example, in November 2011, a magnitude 5.6-earthquake struck near Oklahoma City, which had not experienced such a powerful quake in almost fifty years. St. Gregory's University, near Shawnee, OK, sustained over $1 million of damages, which placed a hefty financial burden on an institution that did not have an emergency plan or earthquake insurance (Basken, 2015). Nearby Oklahoma State University, which is located in the same new frequent earthquake zone, also suffered damages. Retired Senator Jerry Ellis cautioned that if emergency precautions were not put in place soon, the university could face the tragedy of a campus building collapsing (Basken, 2015).

It is advantageous for colleges and universities to create operational safety plans for both natural and manmade disasters. Higher educational institutions reap significant legal, financial, and implementation benefits by doing so. From a legal standpoint, these entities are susceptible to lawsuits (i.e., tort liability) if they do not satisfy a myriad of ever-increasing federal regulatory requirements such as Title IX (i.e., Education Amendments of 1972), Family Educational Rights and Privacy Act (FERPA) (1988), Americans with Disabilities Act (ADA) (1990), and Clery Act (Lipka, 2007; Mumper et al., 2016). The Clery Act, for example, mandates institutions who participate in federal student aid programs to report criminal incidents, such as domestic violence, sexual assaults, stalking, etc., in a timely fashion (Blanchard & Baez, 2016). Institutional staff must then disclose these statistics in an annual security report (Lipka, 2007; Mahaffie, 2014). Under the Clery Act, if it is determined that a college or university failed to notify the campus community of an alleged violation expediently, then the federal government will levy a fine as in the case of Eastern Michigan University (Blanchard & Baez, 2016; U.S. Department of Education, 2007). There, a student was raped and murdered, which eventually cost the university a $350,000 federal fine and a $2.5 million settlement to the victim's family because senior administrators tried to downplay the seriousness of the incident (Blanchard & Baez, 2016; U.S. Department of Education, 2007).

Budgets of colleges and universities are constrained by finite federal funding and state appropriations (Bowen, 2013; Johnstone, 2016; St. John & Parsons, 2004). Higher education institutions compete with K–12 education, health care programs, and corrections because policy makers (i.e., politicians from either political party) prioritize these objectives according to different ideologies regarding what constitutes a public good versus private good (Barr & McClellan, 2017; Johnstone, 2016; St. John & Parsons, 2004). Once a college or university receives their individual appropriation, they then divvy the funds across divisions within the institution. The complexity of encumbering these funds is compounded by a diverse set of obligations such as compliance with research regulations for graduate education, constant upgrades and support for information technology, and enhanced measures for public safety of the campus community (Barr & McClellan, 2017; Bowen, 2013). Public safety divisions for both private and public higher education institutions receive their budget and then divide it to cover overhead costs, training, and preparedness accommodations for disasters (Myers & Lusk, 2017; St. John & Parsons, 2004). While operational safety plans are designed and implemented for the emergency of today, their creators must also account for the ill-defined catastrophe of the future. One example is preparing the physical plant of colleges and universities in coastal regions for between 1.4 and 3.9 feet of sea-level rise by the year 2050 (Myers & Lusk, 2017; NASA JPL, 2019; ODU, 2018c).

One last struggle with the design and implementation of operational safety plans is barricades brought on by politics, disbelief, and communication. When it comes to natural and manmade disasters (e.g., flooding from sea-level rise, active shooter situations, etc.), politicians and the public find it difficult to buy into the idea that "something needs to be done for tomorrow" or individuals struggle to envision the seriousness of potential tragedies. Even if threats are clear, efforts to mitigate damage (i.e., preparation) costs before an event happens may not receive high priority in terms of resources and time (Myers & Lusk, 2017). Therefore, trustworthy information and clear communication from a variety of sources (e.g., meteorologists, law enforcement officials, etc.) need to be at the center of political and educational deliberations when preparing for and responding to unfolding catastrophes (Myers & Lusk, 2017; VCSCS, 2016; Virginia Tech Review Panel, 2007). It is important to note, however, that any discourse, decisions or strategies executed as a crisis unfolds may be altered during a human's response to stress (i.e., the primitive drive for survival overwhelming rational thought) and technological lapses that interrupt communication lines with campus and community stakeholders (Conrad, Galea, Kuroda, & McEwen, 1996; Sapolsky, 1992). While an event is underway, live communication protocols, such as emergency text alerts, intercom messages, and social media announcements, are essential to delivery of instructions that individuals will ideally follow to guide them effectively through a crisis and restore the campus community's sense of well-being (Schildkraut, McKenna, & Elsass, 2017; Sheldon, 2018; Zugazaga, Werner, Clifford, Weaver, & Ware, 2016).

Scholarly literature mainly addresses perceptions on campus safety and little on theoretical underpinnings or necessary components of operational safety plans (Jennings, Gover, & Pudrzynska, 2007; Kaminski, Koons-Witt, Thompson, & Weiss, 2010; Thompson et al., 2009). Due to the diverse and complex nature of potential emergency situations for which a college or university has to prepare, studies have addressed only certain classes of incidents such as property crime, sexual assaults, and mass casualty active shooter situations (Hughes, White, & Hertz, 2008; Schafer, Heiple, Giblin, & Burruss, 2010; Thompson et al., 2009; Zugazaga et al., 2016). Furthermore, analysis of communication strategies has tested the efficacy of certain technologies for potentially mitigating miscommunication (Schildkraut et al., 2017; Sheldon, 2018; Zugazaga et al., 2016). However, these studies lack an underlying theoretical framework that provides either critical analysis regarding the salient factors that enhance design and implementation of operational safety plans or candidate "best practices" for future assessment of plan effectiveness (Dede, Ketelhut, Whitehouse, Breit, & McCloskey, 2009). Furthermore, researchers have rarely employed qualitative or mixed methods research designs, frequently opting for non-experimental quantitative surveys (Asmussen & Creswell, 2013; Patton & Gregory, 2014).

Therefore, this researcher sought to address these gaps in two ways. First, from the literature perspective, the researcher employed open systems organizational theory, supplemented with suppositions from rational choice (manmade) and chaos (natural) theories, in order to better understand how the interplay between institutional mission and external environment produce differences in operational safety plan decisions (Lawrence & Lorsch, 1967; Weick, 1976). Central to the analysis of how an organization designs and implements its operational safety plan was a recognition of "all those significant [environmental] elements outside the organization that influences its ability to survive and achieve its ends" (Scott & Davis, 2007, p. 19). Each institution examined in this study represented unique attributes (e.g., public vs. private, two-year vs. four-year, etc.) that aid in the fulfilling of its organizational goals within certain natural (e.g., rural vs. urban, coastal vs. inland), sociological (e.g., political and legal), and technological (e.g., finances, manpower, equipment, etc.) environmental parameters. Second, from the methodological standpoint, the researcher used qualitative document analysis and interviews in order to identify candidate "best practices," which provided a novel approach to the field of operational safety plan design and implementation (Creswell & Plano Clark, 2011; Lincoln, 2009). By doing so, this critical analysis provided potential recommendations for enhancing organizations' ability to effectively control, mitigate, deter, and reduce future risks associated with manmade and natural disasters (Dede et al., 2009; Fox & Savage, 2009; Randazzo & Plummer, 2009).

THE "WHAT" AND "WHY" OF THIS INVESTIGATION

The purpose of this research study was to discover candidate "best practices" associated with the design and implementation of operational safety plans at college-affiliated institutions. This study included several case studies involving representative higher education and research institutions in the Commonwealth of Virginia. This researcher's objective was to advance understanding of the most effective and salient strategies associated with operational safety plans as well as critical design and implementation factors. The researcher sought to understand what principles guide the design of operational safety plans and what factors were critical for their successful implementation. In answering these questions, the objective was to formulate "best practices" for effective design and implementation of these plans at college-affiliated institutions.

The results drawn from this study, therefore, contributed novel empirical evidence regarding essential components of operational safety plans and how safety personnel at college-affiliated institutions could successfully implement these protocols during crises. Previous research had only examined perceptions of campus safety rather than best practices for design and implementation of these emergency management documents (Baker & Boland, 2011; Kaminski et al., 2010; Patton & Gregory, 2014). Additionally, those studies primarily had been conducted after specific crises, with future readiness for manmade incidents given far more attention than planning for natural disasters (Bonanno & Levenson, 2014; Dow & Cutter, 2000; Jennings et al., 2007; Schafer et al., 2010). As a result, personnel at the nation's colleges, universities, and research institutes are generally left to react "after-the-fact" (Bonanno & Levenson, 2014, p. 1), struggling to maintain control over crisis as it actually unfolds.

Results will be of value to practitioners because they will potentially increase the capability of administrators to manage risks (e.g., financial loss, civil liability, etc.). Higher education institutions and their affiliates can experience substantial disruptions to their operations because of crises, which can affect finances, morale, and academic life (Dietz, 2017; Oliver, 2009; Waugh, 2004). For example, in the aftermath of the 2007 Virginia Tech mass shooting, the university paid out roughly $48 million, which included $100,000 to each victim's family for medical and mental-health expenses (Johnson, 2012; Lipka, 2008; Randazzo & Plummer, 2009). To address deficiencies revealed by the Virginia Tech incident, the Commonwealth of Virginia (2008) mandated that all higher education institutions have an operational safety plan, including a contingency plan for active shooter scenarios. However, there remains no clear guidelines regarding "best practices" for the design and implementation of these plans.

Given that most of the applicable literature was descriptive in nature with only a single proposed conceptual framework, this researcher offered a novel theoretical approach to understanding the research problem of interest (Baker & Boland, 2011; Patton & Gregory, 2014; Schafer et al., 2010; Thompson et al., 2009). Open Systems Theory examines how organizations (e.g., college-affiliated institutions) integrate with the patterns and structures of their environments in order to meet requirements necessary for economic, political, and social survival (Scott & Davis, 2007; Weick, 1976). By using this approach, the study offered a new robust explanatory perspective that could lead to future design-based research that will further advance the field's understanding of "best practices" for design and implementation of operational safety plans.

INVESTIGATING THE "WHO, WHEN, WHERE, AND HOW" FOR THIS STUDY

This qualitative exploratory research project employed a comparative case study methodology because of its appropriateness for answering the proposed research questions (Berg, 2001; Creswell, 2013; Creswell & Plano Clark, 2011). To address the knowledge gap in this field of research, a systematic analysis of operational safety planning documents inductively yielded insights into essential principles and factors potentially necessary for successfully responding to a wide range of natural and manmade incidents (Creswell, 2013; Strauss & Corbin, 1998). Furthermore, case studies can provide researchers with an opportunity to collect data that increases understanding of a general occurrence (i.e., design and implementation of operational safety plans), which extends beyond the boundaries of that particular research (Stake, 2000; Yin, 2018). In this research project, several representative sites were purposefully selected to show how different environments can lead to different impacts on the design and implementation of operational safety plans. Thus, the researcher's objective in this study was to outline evidence-based "best practices" and to make recommendations that can enhance the design and implementation of future emergency operational safety plans for college-affiliated institutions. Findings may also eventually be applicable to understanding operational safety planning for organizations beyond higher education (Creswell, 2013).

"Who" participated? The population from which the sample was drawn includes higher education and research institutions. The researcher purposefully selected based on either of the following two criteria: 1) the Virginia state legislature mandated in 2008 that institutions create threat assessment teams (Virginia 23-9.2:10 [effective March 7, 2008] and 23.1-805 [effective October 1, 2016]), or 2) accreditation from Emergency Management Accreditation Program (EMAP) (Berg, 2001; Creswell, 2013). The sample included the following five organizations: two public universities (Idaho State University and Old Dominion University), one public two-year college (Tidewater Community College), one hybrid graduate school-research center (Eastern Virginia Medical School), and one research center (NASA Langley Research Center). The data from these institutions provided insight into how different organizational requirements (i.e., mission and objectives) and environments affect decisions regarding design and implementation of operational safety plans. Four of the five selected institutions experience unique natural disasters that institutions further inland do not have to plan for (i.e., sea-level rise, hurricanes, etc.). These institutions were compared to the fifth, which represented a benchmark because of an EMAP accreditation that the others do not possess.

"How" was the Investigation Conducted? The researcher collected operational safety plans from the selected institutions and read each one in order to perform open, descriptive coding that identified various components (i.e., candidate "best practices") for responding to natural and manmade disasters (Berg, 2001; Creswell, 2013; Maxwell, 2005). After the collection of codes, data were pooled and analyzed in aggregate in order to construct overall themes. These results provided insight or guidance into future quantitative research that could bolster support for the "best practices" elucidated in this study (Suen, Lei, & Li, 2012).

INVESTIGATIVE BOUNDARIES

Several boundaries (i.e., delimitations) were put in place as part of this study's qualitative research design. Most importantly, this research focused primarily on operational safety plan and related documents (e.g., advisories issued during an emergency). While every organization has them, there was little to no research available in the literature benchmarking what constituted "best practices" for these safety documents. Moreover, salient to the qualitative document analysis, this study only selected operational safety plans from college-affiliated institutions within the Commonwealth of Virginia, plus Idaho State University. This region was utilized due to its institutional diversity, as well as the potential for coastal natural disasters that do not affect inland locations with the same severity. Idaho State University was included because of its status as an EMAP-certified institution, which represented a blue light standard to compare the other institutions to (EMAP, 2019).

Institutions were selected for case study analysis due to their unique circumstances. For example, candidate organizations included a public university that was proactive in planning for natural disasters, and a public two-year college that had to update its operational safety plan following a potential active shooter situation. In addition, this research examined a

restricted access government facility used by U.S. college-affiliated institutions as well as a public four-year specialty graduate school because of
their need to protect research assets. By imposing a geographical constraint,
the study intentionally selected these organizations in order to document
how an institution's distinctive mission and its external environment could
influence decisions regarding the design and implementation of operational
safety plans for natural and manmade disasters.

Chapter One

Higher Education Institutions as Organizations

OPEN SYSTEMS

Colleges and universities are organizations that impact and are influenced by the social structures of society, their attributes, and processes (Luhman & Cunliffe, 2013; Scott & Davis, 2007). Lawrence and Lorsch (1967) conceptualized these complex collectivities that can initiate change as:

> A system of interrelated behaviors of people who are performing a task that has been differentiated into several distinct subsystems each subsystem performing a portion of the task, and the efforts of each being integrated to achieve effective performance of the system. (p. 3)

Within every environment, there are many organizations; their shared relationships vary among three conceptual perspectives: rational, natural, and open systems. Among these perspectives, open systems posit the highest degree of economic, political, or social interaction between an organization and its environment (Luhman & Cunliffe, 2013; Scott & Davis, 2007; Weick, 1976). With respect to the external environment, Scott and Davis (2007) conceptualize that:

> Every organization exists in a specific physical, technological, cultural, and social environment to which it must adapt. No organization is self-sufficient; all depend for survival on the types of relations they establish with the larger systems of which they are a part. Environments are all those significant elements outside the organization that influences its ability to survive and achieve its ends. The environment can be seen as a store of resources as well as a source of opportunities and constraints, demands, and threats. It includes the clients, constituents, or customers that the organization serves and the providers of resources it requires to do so. (pp. 19–20)

11

For higher education institutions and their affiliates, a paramount environmental element to consider when examining operational safety plans is the organizational town and gown relationship (i.e., how well do college/university leadership collaborate with municipal leaders and first responders) (EMAP, 2016). Depending on the scope of a natural or manmade disaster, campus safety personnel may need to rely on community resources to adequately cope with the crisis. For example, the sheer magnitude of the mass shooting at Virginia Tech (VT) University on April 16, 2007, forced the VT Police Department to request assistance from federal and state law enforcement agencies. In the aftermath of this crisis, the Commonwealth of Virginia convened a panel to investigate what led Cho to act in this manner and what steps could be taken to ensure that something like it never happened again (Virginia Tech Review Panel, 2007). Among its findings, the panel recommended that the Commonwealth legislatively mandate the creation of operational safety plans and threat assessment teams for all educational institutions (legislative Code of Virginia 23-9.2:10 [effective March 7, 2008] and 23.1-805 [effective October 1, 2016]). Although that disaster represented an extreme in terms of consensus or buy-in (i.e., opening of a "policy window" that allowed legislative policy to be enacted), state and federal political forces operating in an institution's external environment can have a significant impact on the organization's ability to design and implement operational safety plans (EMAP, 2016; Theodoulou & Kofinis, 2004). This task is one of many goal objectives that a higher education institution needs to meet, each of which require task-specific hardware, financial resources, and qualified worker expertise (Duryea, 1973; Orlikowski, 1992; Scott & Davis, 2007). The task environment, as it relates to implementation and execution of future operational safety plans, ". . . emphasizes those features of the environment relevant to its supply of inputs and its disposition of outputs but also includes the power-dependent relations within which the organization conducts its exchanges" (Scott & Davis, 2007, p. 125). Risk assessment and mitigation, therefore, entails the evaluating, prioritizing, and coordinating of resources available in a complex, dynamic external environment (Dow & Cutter, 2000; EMAP, 2016; Sheldon, 2018).

In order to run an organization, administrators obtain demands (e.g., political and financial) from the environment and thus create policy, which outlines goals and plans (i.e., stakeholders' expectations for campus safety) (Baker & Boland, 2011; Scott & Davis, 2007; Swinth, 1974). These objectives are then filtered through a controlling division (i.e., senior administrators and campus safety police chiefs), which takes the raw material and transforms it into products and services (e.g., operational safety plans) (Scott & Davis, 2007; Swinth, 1974; Thompson, Price, Mrdjenovich, & Khubchandani, 2009). Although researchers hypothesize that organizations operate as open systems, colleges and universities differ slightly due to goal ambiguity, a diffuse locus of control across multiple groups of professional staffs, and environmental vulnerability (Baldridge, Curtis, Ecker, & Riley, 1977).

Scott and Davis (2007) argued that open system organizations are loosely coupled, hierarchical and complex systems much like higher educational institutions. Researchers argue that colleges and universities obtain their resources through the environment to assist in self-maintaining (Glassman, 1973). Furthermore, in deciding where and how much to allocate those environmental resources, administrators of loosely coupled systems select from among groups of individuals that are slightly or occasionally connected across different sub-divisions for the purpose of achieving one or two main missions. Since these clusters may be interrelated to varying degrees (i.e., a hierarchical system), higher education institutions rely on management to coordinate these complex interactions toward meeting organizational goals and objectives (Scott & Davis, 2007).

When applying open system organizations and their characteristics to a college or university's operational safety planning policy, one may recognize that personnel and assorted equipment (i.e., environmental resources) are needed to self-maintain the emergency safety strategy. In designating different units (e.g., senior administrators, chief of police and his or her staff, etc.) to contribute their expertise toward the overall operational safety planning, it is important to note that, although connected, they are loosely coupled by virtue of their different responsibilities, which may be only slightly or occasionally connected to achievement of the institution's overall mission. Furthermore, the nature and extent of these selected individuals' contributions to effective emergency planning depends on perceived and actual authority attributed to these groups based on their position within a complex hierarchical structure (Lawrence & Lorsch, 1967).

Given the internal complexity of colleges and universities and the myriad of environments those institutions must operate in, contingency theory affords one theoretical lens through which to understand how operational safety plans come about in open systems (Scott & Davis, 2007). Lawrence and Lorsch (1967) first observed that different environments would place entirely different demands on organizations (in this study, higher education institutions), which would respond with varying degrees of structure, members' interpersonal orientation toward colleagues, and their time and goal orientations. With different classifications (private vs. public, two-year vs. four-year, suburban vs. urban, coastal vs. inland, etc.), colleges and universities differentiate their operational units into structural features with more (or less) formal structure and more (or less) centralized decision-making (Scott & Davis, 2007). For operational safety plans, this entails the participation of at least the administrative and campus safety units, each of which has a unique identity within the organization and relationship with internal and external stakeholders. However, these units must also integrate in order to meet the organizational task of creating and successfully implementing an operational safety plan in a moment of natural or manmade crisis. As must be noted though, the relationship between their ". . . differentiation and integration are essentially antagonistic, and that one can be obtained only at the expense of the other" (Lawrence & Lorsch, 1967, p. 47). The inherent challenge is finding a "best fit" (Scott & Davis, 2007, p. 103) that satisfies the unique character of an educational institution and its external environment. Contingency theory is useful in understanding how a higher education institution (i.e., organization) might adapt its emergency management operations to indeterminate and rapid environmental changes, but this framework does not entirely account for why having a "final" version of an operational safety plan may be nearly impossible.

Weick (1976) posited in his theoretical model that an organization (e.g., higher education institution) can be a set of loosely and tightly coupled subsystems. In a tightly coupled subsystem, essential personnel such as senior administrators, safety police personnel, full-time faculty, senate team, etc. contribute their expertise to the design and implementation of an operational safety plan that is unique to their organizational needs and mission intended to keep people safe (Scott & Davis, 2007). On the other hand, in a loosely coupled subassembly, regardless of their expertise and planning, the execution (i.e., actions) of an emergency safety plan may fall short of their intentions, leaving administrators frustrated (Glassman, 1973; March, 1981; Weick, 1976). While applying Weick's (1976) suppositions help to make sense of organizational dynamics among administrators, safety experts and the community, which is to be protected by an operational safety plan, this theoretical model does not adequately address the diversity of college-affiliated organizations and their differing structures, which may or may not be as loosely coupled as Weick proposed.

OPERATIONAL PLANS' THEORETICAL FRAMEWORKS

Manmade Disasters

In studies of operational safety planning, there are little to no theoretical frameworks that researchers use to guide their inquiries. The closest conceptual framework was that of Thompson, Price, Mrdjenovich, & Khubchandani (2009)'s model: Reducing firearm-related violence on college campuses. This framework was designed from a public health perspective, which the authors provided three levels of prevention on firearm violence (i.e., morbidity and mortality) on a college campus (i.e., Primary, Secondary, and Tertiary levels). Under these preventive levels, the goals are to keep firearms from being brought onto a college campus, the creation of protocols for reporting gun safety and theft issues, and that a communication systems and relevant training should be in place if a firearm related incident does occur. However, Thompson et al.'s (2009) model has yet to be empirically tested to verify the validity of any of the three levels in preventing or mitigating a type of manmade disaster.

What may, however, answer the "why" a person commits violence at a college-affiliated institution or anywhere else for that matter is the work of Marcus Felson and Lawrence Cohen. They proposed Rational Choice Theory, which states that individuals do not commit crime based on biological, psychological, or environmental factors. Rather "people voluntarily, willfully choose to commit criminal acts such as burglary, car theft, and assault just like they willfully choose to do other things, such as work in a grocery store, go to college, or use recreational drugs" (Criminal Justice, 2019, p. 2). Bouffard and Exum (2013) posited that Rational Choice Theory assumes that all people are rational who calculate and weigh their decisions based on perceived benefit or satisfaction to increase pleasure or profit. For example, Bouffard and Exum (2013) surveyed undergraduate students and convicted felons on a hypothetical drunk driving scenario. Respondents answered a series of rational choice questions pertaining to costs and benefits of driving drunk and the authors concluded that regardless of respondents' status, individuals calculated their decisions to commit a crime (e.g., drunk drinking). Other studies have shown that offenders committed crimes based on the expected costs and reward of offending (i.e., the expected payoff for committing a crime) (Cornish & Clarke, 1986; Grasmick & Bursik, 1990; Kubrin, Stucky, & Krohn, 2009).

Such costs may include state fines and incarceration, social embarrassment or loss of respect, and self-imposed shame and guilt (Grasmick & Bursik, 1990; Porter, 2013; Saraga, 2008). To illustrate, Whitman (1998) argued that shame sanction's main idea is to humiliate an offender and hope to prevent them from repeating the same mistake and for those who have not offended from ever being arrested (Porter, 2013). An application of this concept is the State of Ohio shame-sanctioning program where the issuance of a yellow with red letter license plate was legally mandated for all drivers who presented a blood alcohol content of .17 or higher and those repeat offenders (Porter, 2013). Longitudinal research has confirmed that informal punishments (i.e., Ohio's yellow plates) can be a successful way to deter drunken driving violations (Grasmick, Bursik, & Arneklev, 1993; Porter, 2013).

Thus, Rational Choice Theory may prove useful in the design of operational safety plans in that students appear to be more responsive to a crime's "costs" and less likely to commit them due to "greater social bonds/capital to risk when contemplating crime and, therefore, need a larger perceived incentive to engage in criminal behavior" (Bouffard & Exum, 2013, p. 446). When examining the Virginia Tech massacre, the Review Panel (2007) found that Cho was socially isolated and university officials had difficulty in providing treatment assistance to him that would have provided some kind of social capital/structure. Under Rational Choice Theory, Cho would have weighed the costs and benefits of his actions. However, shame and guilt from disrupting his almost non-existent social bonds were not costs to him and thus did not deter Cho from shooting two people in West Ambler Johnston, leaving campus to mail his manifesto, and then returning to chain the doors of Norris Hall shut so he could kill an additional thirty individuals (Virginia Tech Panel, 2007). This example demonstrates the potential utility in applying Rational Choice Theory to understanding how manmade crises may occur at colleges, universities, and their affiliates, and guide planners in selecting strategies for mitigating and deterring them.

Natural Disasters

As with operational safety planning for manmade events, there are few theoretical frameworks available for researchers to apply when examining the design process for natural crises. Such events are highly unpredictable because they result from complex earth systems, which are inherently dynamic and seemingly impossible to control. However, they can cost a college or university millions (or billions) of dollars in damage and lost revenue (Basken, 2015; United States Department of Homeland Security, 2006). While it may not be entirely necessary for administrators and campus safety personnel to know what exactly triggers an earthquake or tornado from a scientific perspective, the fact that the seeming chaos can have predictable patterns (i.e., expecting the unexpected) may assist them with selecting strategies that mitigate adverse effects from meteorological, geological, and oceanographic events to their institutions.

Most of twentieth-century science (e.g., physics, meteorology, economics, etc.) has focused on reducing systems down to their components in the hopes that if all parts were identified and their relationships characterized, then scientists would be able to understand the original complete system (Gleick, 2008; Lawrence & Lorsch, 1967). However, most researchers acknowledged that some measure of uncertainty or error had to be introduced into their descriptions or calculations, resulting in approximations (Gleick, 2008). The more complex the system, the less the approximation might match actual events. Thus, there were certain phenomena (e.g., weather forecasting) that appeared to be beyond the reach of inquiry because of their apparent irregularity or chaotic nature (De Domenico, Ghorbani, Makarynskyy, Makarynska, & Asadi, 2013; Gleick, 2008; Scheidegger, 1997).

At issue is how humans approach knowledge and inquiry (Fish, 1989; Mackey, 1995). By breaking information into academic disciplines (e.g., criminal justice) and simplifying it, humans have imposed an arbitrary order on the world that is useful only to a point (Fish, 1989). While these tendencies are most helpful in teaching and learning, it cannot capture the true complexity and randomness of nature, including human behavior (normal, deviant or criminal) (Mackey, 1995). For example, traditional ("Euclidean") geometry deals with "smooth" shapes (i.e., lines, circles, triangles) that lend themselves to fairly straightforward mathematical analysis (Mandelbrot, 1982; NOVA, 2008). However, these smooth shapes are not commonly found in the real world (e.g., mountains, coastlines, etc.) and, therefore, researchers require a different kind of analytical tool: the visual representations of complexity produced by fractal geometry (Gleick, 2008; Mandelbrot, 1982). Thus, Chaos Theory and fractal geometry challenge traditional boundaries of thought, forcing those who ascribe to it to approach global problems in an interdisciplinary manner (Donald, 2009; Gleick, 2008; Poole, 2009).

Chaos theory deals with identifying repeatable patterns in extremely complex systems that appear to be disordered to human beings. To illustrate, Chaos Theory is mostly associated with the butterfly effect; that is, a butterfly flapping its wings in Virginia Beach, VA, will affect whether it rains or shines in Naples, Italy (Gleick, 2008). When a butterfly flaps its wings, it creates tiny variations in atmospheric air molecules and microscopic pollutants that may trigger the conditions necessary for rain cloud formation. Water vapor cannot form a cloud unless it has a substrate (i.e., microscopic pollutant, dust particle, water, sea salt, etc.) to condense around (Ludlam, 1948). As the microscopic particles collide with one another, they coalesce into the large white cloud structure that can be seen with the human eye (Gleick, 2008; Ludlam, 1948). With the increase in airborne pollution over the last several decades, there now exists one more variable to account for in weather forecasting computer models that draw on what has been learned from chaos and fractal geometry (Gleick, 2008; Myers & Lusk, 2017; Rasmussen, 2019).

Understanding randomness and Chaos Theory can aid emergency management planners as they prepare their campuses for a variety of meteorological, geological, and oceanographic situations (Inskeep, 2019; Myers & Lusk, 2017). This is not to say that emergency planners must be experts themselves in the underlying science of chaos and fractal geometry, but rather that they have an appreciation for its importance in enhancing human capabilities to predict, plan, and prepare before natural disasters strike (Inskeep, 2019; Rasmussen, 2019). By being scientifically literate, institutional leaders become empowered through a fundamental awareness that better forecasting and predictions lead to better emergency planning (Basken, 2015; Inskeep, 2019; United States Department of Homeland Security, 2006).

Operational Safety Plan Analysis

Sutcliffe (2018) postulated that "Crisis management scholarship arguably has struggled for decades to find a central place in management and organization theory" (p. 486). Regardless of whether one is discussing a multinational corporation, an educational institution or an informal group of people protesting a cause, all are considered an organization (Scott & Davis, 2007), which contributed to the rationale for utilizing Open Systems Theory in this research as the primary framework. This philosophy (i.e., Open Systems Theory) allowed the researcher to potentially account for influences of unique environments when reviewing operational safety plans from a diverse set of higher education and their affiliated organizations. In other words, the document analysis protocol theme, *Training*, may have been present in each institution's operational safety plan, but may have been implemented differently from one institution to another (see appendix A).

As one of two secondary frameworks, Rational Choice Theory was utilized because people rationally calculate the costs and benefits of a particular plan of action (Dow & Cutter, 2000; Ford & Frei, 2016; Sheldon, 2018). For example, "people voluntarily, willfully choose to commit criminal acts . . . just like they willfully choose to do other things, such as . . ." (Criminal Justice, 2019, p. 2) acknowledging text alerts and sirens issued for natural or manmade disasters. This philosophy allows the research to understand the rationale behind individuals' decision making in a crisis situation, which may be accounted for within segments of an institution's operational safety plan that were classified under the document analysis protocol *Communication* theme (see appendix A).

The other secondary framework used in this research was Chaos Theory, which deals with identifying repeatable patterns in extremely complex systems that appear to be disordered to human beings. This theory acknowledges the predictability of natural disasters before they happen, and then what to do during and in their aftermath. For example, this creates the opportunity for complex computer modeling and simulation that give emergency planners the means to plan and practice for these horrific events such items that fell under the *Training, Resources, Emergency Management, and Communication* protocol themes (see appendix A).

Chapter Two

Emergency Management Planning

To deal with hazards from crisis, emergency management planning involves coordination and integration of local, state, and federal response teams, which are essential to mitigate and recover from both natural and manmade incidents (International Association of Emergency Managers [IAEM], 2007; Waugh, 2003). Depending on the scope of the disaster, emergency management planners must activate first responders, emergency support functions (e.g., food and health care), and rescue equipment (Waugh, 2003). Once a catastrophic event is over and life returns to normal, emergency planners can review what went well or not in order to enhance future emergency safety operations.

According to the International Association of Emergency Managers [IAEM] (2007), "emergency management is the managerial function charged with creating the framework within which communities reduce vulnerability to hazards and cope with disasters" (p. 4). Planners must determine what is or is not a crisis (i.e., consists of an element of surprise, poses a threat to public safety, disrupts normal operations, etc.) by conducting a comprehensive risk assessment of potential hazards to occur within a given area, including determination of impact severity and probability of transpiring (Bataille & Cordova, 2014; IAEM, 2007; Zdiarski, Dunkel, & Rollo, 2007). Before any crisis occurs, local agencies will develop an emergency plan that takes into consideration unique issues created by these catastrophic events as well as their effects on residents and businesses. As part of this emergency plan, local emergency management may identify state and federal agencies to collaborate with during incident responses (Federal Emergency Management Agency [FEMA], 2011a; IAEM, 2007).

Federal agencies have a shared responsibility with local organizations when responding to any natural or manmade catastrophe, although how critical an incident is determines which one takes primary lead in coordinating the necessary means to address the crisis (Dow & Cutter, 2000; Waugh, 2003). Prior to the September 11 attacks, public agencies, nonprofit, and private organizations worked together to provide relief services for natural and technological (i.e., manmade) disasters (FEMA, 2011b; Waugh, 2003). This National Emergency Management Network (NEMN) was formalized by the Nunn-Lugar-Domenici (i.e., Defense Against Weapons of Mass Destruction Act of 1996), which allocated financial resources for equipment and training of local first responders to handle terrorist attacks in their communities (Bauman, 2017; Waugh, 2003). Shortly thereafter, in 1997, Congress passed a reauthorization of the National Defense Authorization Act by which the Department of Defense (DOD) converted its 1208 program into the 1033 program that made surplus military equipment available for purchase to all law enforcement agencies across the countries for counter-drug and counter-terrorism efforts (Bauman, 2017; Kealy, 2003; Kraska, 2007). In the years leading up to 9/11 and in the aftermath of such events as the Oklahoma City bombing (1995) and the TWA Flight 800 crash (1996), policy makers envisioned emergency management planning from a local perspective with substantial federal assistance in preparation for any terrorism act. While natural disasters did occur (e.g., Hurricane Andrew [1992]) within this timeframe, the primary focus of emergency planners was on manmade disasters (Dow & Cutter, 2000; Tonry & Farrington, 1995; Waugh, 2003).

Post 9/11, the focus became even heavier on manmade catastrophes at the federal level when those agencies conducted emergency management planning through the lens of a law enforcement perspective with its command-and-control orientation (FEMA, 2011; Waugh, 2003). As one example, these agencies shared and received information globally between intelligence and law enforcement, giving emergency management more of a prosecutorial role than true planning purpose (Monahan, 2010; Oliver, 2009; Vervaele, 2005). With passage of the U.S. Patriot Act in 2001, the intelligence-sharing procedures for FBI intelligence and counter-intelligence were broadened to include provision of any pertinent information "that is necessary to the ability of the U.S. to investigate or protect against attack, sabotage, terrorism, and clandestine intelligence activities" (Vervaele, 2005, p. 420) to the U.S. Attorney General's Office. According to Monahan (2010), intelligence-gathering agencies (e.g., FBI, CIA, NSA, etc.) expanded their domestic surveillance efforts in the wake of the September 11 attacks, although many of these programs existed in some form for many years prior to this particular manmade disaster (Wood, Konvitz, & Ball, 2003). Thus, state and local officials have deferred toward the Department of Homeland Security (DHS) (i.e., federal government) in organizing preparation and response efforts to manmade disasters, especially terrorist attacks (Becker, 2004; Oliver, 2009; Waugh, 2003). For example, Becker (2004) described a multiyear study, the Pre-Event Message Development Project, in which the Centers for Disease Control and Prevention (CDC), the National Institute for Occupational Safety and Health (NIOSH), and several higher education institutions obtained feedback from focus groups regarding information needs and preferred communication methods during a hypothetical nuclear-radiological terrorist attack. Researchers collected data from 163 individuals participating in either general public (n=12) or first responder (n=4) focus groups across multiple U.S. geographic regions (Becker, 2004). While the public preferred clear information for staying healthy and safe during a nuclear terrorist emergency, first responders indicated concerns about self-protection, threats of being targeted, etc. (Becker, 2004; Becker, 2010; Veenema, Walden, Feinstein, & Williams, 2008). CDC and NIOSH personnel used this study's results to improve emergency communication protocols. Other research after 9/11 mirrored the federal government's unilateral decision to exert centralized command-and-control over all aspects of emergency management planning, despite a reliance on local agencies to communicate and execute those responses (Becker, 2004; Oliver, 2009).

A natural disaster on the scale of Hurricane Katrina in 2005, however, exposed the inevitable weaknesses of viewing emergency management planning from a federal law enforcement perspective (Monahan, 2010; Oliver, 2009; Waugh, 2003). Law enforcement agencies have a tendency to not share information and act as though their intelligence is proprietary in nature (Waugh, 2003). Furthermore, law enforcement decision makers operate based on an enforcement and prosecutorial standpoint, which covers manmade disasters well; what law enforcement personnel cannot do is show a hurricane or a tornado their badges and expect it to cease (Oliver, 2009; Tonry & Farrington, 1995; Waugh, 2003). Katrina was one of the deadliest hurricanes ever to hit the United States (DHS, 2006; National Weather Service, 2016). Even though no one could have predicted the impact brought on by Hurricane Katrina and the ensuing aftermath, there are challenges brought on when a natural disaster is considered with the same law enforcement philosophy as a manmade crisis. In fact, according to Cooper and Block (2006), the Department of Homeland Security's emergency planning for natural disasters, especially as it related to Hurricane Katrina, was an "abject failure" (p. xiii). Recognizing the centralized, law enforcement focus on terrorism by DHS over the past several years, emergency planners frantically tried to warn of unpreparedness and inadequate planning procedures for a natural catastrophe as Katrina approached:

> The Department of Homeland Security was to be the embodiment of federal might, sharpened to a fine point. It would be a "good" bureaucracy, designed to coordinate all federal disasters efforts into a single, focused, modern machine. But this proved not to be the case at all . . . all manner of emergency responders

who had watched helplessly for years as Bush administration officials summarily dismantled the Federal Emergency Management Agency and remade it into a cadre of debris janitors and political hacks. (Cooper & Block, 2006, pp. xiv-xv)

Federal reorganization of emergency management agencies under George W. Bush was merely the latest episode in a series of misappropriations and reclaiming of monies that left the City of New Orleans less prepared for natural disasters, especially hurricanes. In fact, throughout several presidential administrations, including those of Ronald Reagan and Bill Clinton, funds were allocated to other projects in Louisiana, such as the Red River Navigation Project shipping channel connecting Shreveport to the Mississippi River at a cost of $2 billion (Cooper & Block, 2006). Reallocating these resources toward repairing and upgrading New Orleans' defenses (e.g., pump stations, levees, drainage canals, etc.) that can withstand hurricanes, flooding, heavy winds, etc. might have been more effective, especially since previous storms had already revealed weaknesses in the city's decaying severe weather infrastructure (Cooper & Block, 2006; Cowen & Seifter, 2018; Johnson & Rainey, 2007; van Heerden & Bryan, 2006). State and local malfeasance occurred with Sewerage & Water Board as well as the Levee Board when these members collected millage taxes to maintain the city's pump stations, levees, etc. However, they inappropriately used the funds toward land development of swamp and back marshes surrounding New Orleans, reducing the City's natural defenses against storm surge (Cooper & Block, 2006). Furthermore, graft and corruption were also taking its toll; for example, James Huey, president of the Levee Board, skimmed $100,000 of its funds for personal gain (i.e., money that was supposed to be used for emergency management planning) (Cooper & Block, 2006).

In the months leading up to Hurricane Katrina, federal funds were mostly distributed to training and preparedness activities associated with manmade (e.g., Islamic jihadist terrorist attacks) disasters. Specifically, the Department of Homeland Security personnel gave funds through their Office of State and Local Government Coordination and Preparedness to "detect, prevent, and disrupt terrorist attack . . . rarely [to deal] with natural calamities" (Cooper & Block, 2006, p. 12). One exception was the awarding of DHS funds in 2004 to plan for a natural disaster. Several key components to this exercise were 1) the inclusion of federal, state and local planners, 2) situating the scenario in a high-populated area prone to flooding, and 3) use of a simulation called Hurricane Pam (Cooper & Block, 2006). Researchers and planners frequently utilize computer-based simulations to isolate and examine in-depth variables that have complex relationships with each other and the situation under study (Briggs & Kennedy, 2016 Gleick, 2008; Myers & Lusk, 2017; Rasmussen, 2019). For example, the National Transportation Safety Board (NTSB) used computer simulations in order to determine whether pilot Chesley "Sully" Sullenberger made the best decision *after* he landed Flight 1549 on the Hudson River following dual engine loss (Sullenberger, 2009). Additionally, *during* Apollo 13, ground crews simulated what the astronauts were experiencing in space when an unexpected explosion crippled their spacecraft so that the crew could safely power up their command module and parachutes before re-entering Earth's atmosphere (Cortright, 1970; Dumoulin, 2001; NASA, 2018). Simulations constructed *during* and *after* a major event tend to have a greater believability since the majority of variables are known.

In the Hurricane Pam simulation, which was conducted *before* Hurricane Katrina ever came into existence, emergency planners failed to account for all possible impacts of a category 3 hurricane in New Orleans (Cooper & Block, 2006). In fact, it had been over thirty years since Louisiana had experienced a direct hit from a hurricane. Computer simulations have their limitations because humans sometimes fail to account for critical variables or are over-confident in their ability to handle situations. Computer simulations in Sully's case, for example, initially showed that he could have landed safely at an airport, which ultimately was shown not to be the case because NTSB investigators failed to include the human variable (i.e., the time it took the pilots to assess what happened and possible alternatives before making a decision) (Sullenberger, 2009). In Apollo 13, the ground crew initially failed to account for extra power usage by the lunar module after the accident, which would have depleted the batteries far faster and led to loss of the crew long before they ever returned to Earth (Cortright, 1970; Dumoulin, 2001; NASA, 2018). Once engineers caught the oversight, they were able to include that variable during their simulations that ultimately saved the astronauts. In the Hurricane Pam simulation, state and local emergency personnel believed FEMA officials when they promised that they would help to fill in the gaps during an emergency. However, when later simulations and emergency planning sessions were scheduled to finish hurricane preparations, DHS failed to appropriate the funds necessary to send FEMA representatives needed for successful collaboration between federal, state, and local officials during natural disaster incidents (Cooper & Block, 2006). As a result, emergency planners were not prepared when Hurricane Katrina came ashore in August 2005 with its devastating effects.

In conclusion, emergency management planning ideally involves the integration of local, state, and federal response teams in the event of a natural or manmade catastrophe. However, the necessary means for these agencies to collaborate has shifted the power to DHS, FEMA, and other federal agencies. Prior to 9/11, state and local governments took the lead in emergency management planning for natural and manmade disasters with the assistance of federal surplus equipment and grant funding. Post 9/11, federal agencies imposed their power (i.e., organizational ranking) and took on the lead role in major catastrophes. Congress enacted the Patriot Act of 2001, establishing DHS with a command-and-control organizational structure that changed emergency planning into a law enforcement activity focused on terrorism. However, as Waugh (2003) predicted two years prior to Hurricane Katrina, this new emergency management network approach did not function as well as its creators intended when New Orleans flooded. While emergency planners could have taken Hurricane Katrina as a warning to elevate the importance of preparing for natural disasters to the same level as they did for manmade crises, those lessons, however, got lost when an active shooter took the lives of thirty-two individuals at Virginia Tech in 2007.

HIGHER EDUCATION EMERGENCY OPERATIONAL PREPAREDNESS

There are a number of articles that address college emergency preparedness for operational safety plans (Asmussen & Creswell, 2013; Kaminski, Koons-Witt, Thompson, & Weiss, 2010; Shafer, Heiple, Giblin, & Burruss, 2010; Thompson, Price, Mrdjenovich, & Khubchandani, 2009). Some of the major themes in this literature are early intervention, coordination with outside agencies, and leadership and governance (FEMA, 2015; National Center for Campus Public Safety, 2016a; Traynor, 2012; Zugazaga, Werner, Clifford, Weaver, & Ware, 2016). Furthermore, the literature in this area once again focuses primarily on manmade crises (e.g., active shooter, violent crimes, etc.) (Asmussen & Creswell, 2013; Baker & Boland, 2001; Dahl, Bonham, & Reddington, 2016). Even though there is a research emphasis on effective strategies for responding to violent campus threats, a few studies in this literature base report findings related to stakeholders' perceptions on how safe they feel on campus, which is useful information when designing and implementing operational safety plans for both natural and manmade disasters (Hughes, White, & Hertz, 2008; Jennings, Gover, & Pudrzynska, 2007; Lannon, 2014; Shafer, Heiple, Giblin, & Burruss, 2010; Thompson et al., 2009; Zugazaga, Werner, Clifford, Weaver, & Ware, 2016).

HIGHER EDUCATION LEADERSHIP AND GOVERNANCE

College and university officials can help or hinder the design and implementation of operational safety plans for their institutions by promoting emergency awareness (GAO, 2018). Administrators can encourage stakeholders to "buy-in" (GAO, 2018, p. 10) through their commitment to a culture of safety by providing the means and time for everyone to participate in needed training, webinars, conferences, etc. (Richardson, 1994). A college president, in particular, sets the tone for the entire campus community to follow and as such becomes the public face of that college or university; in fact, Eckel (2015) stated that, "no leader comes to personify an institution in the way a president does . . ." (p. 161). To illustrate, at Michigan State University, college president Lou Anna K. Simon allegedly set a "culture of indifference" (Stripling, 2019, p. 8) toward sexual assault. Staff at the University Women's Resource Center perceived that President Simon did not make the issue of sexual assault a priority by not adequately funding and staffing the facility. For example, the program was housed in a "creepy-looking" basement and staffed by two therapists and one prevention counselor for 50,000 students despite multiple pleas for additional resources (Stripling, 2019, p. 9). On the opposite side of the spectrum, Dr. Steve Sample, President of the University of Southern California (USC), set a positive institutional culture through upgrading the quality of the student body by admitting top level applicants, recruiting top ranked faculty, expanding USC's global presence through collaborations with other universities (i.e., Association of Pacific Rim Universities), and strengthening relationships with communities in the Los Angeles area in the aftermath of the 1992 riots (Cowen & Seifter, 2018).

Leadership and governing boards work together to meet federal requirements and reduce tort liability issues when developing operational safety plans (Blanchard & Baez, 2016). While operational safety plans need to address all kinds of unexpected situations, federal and state statutes are particularly relevant to students who are a threat to themselves or others. University CARE and threat assessment teams aid in deterring incidents from happening in the first place by identifying at-risk individuals under Virginia code sections 19.2-389 or 16.1-301. Family Educational Rights and Privacy Act (FERPA) normally does not grant higher education officials access to students' education records (e.g., disabilities or mental health status), although a student may voluntarily disclose that information for the purpose of being granted appropriate accommodations and support (FERPA, 1988). If he or she does so, Americans with Disabilities Act (ADA) protects them from being discriminated against based on their disabilities. However, at least in the state of Virginia, state code grants special permission to university officials to run a background (section 19.2-389) and juvenile (section 16.1-301) records check if someone is deemed a threat (i.e., articulable reason) (Pena, 2008).

As a crisis unfolds, two additional federal laws guide execution of major components in operational safety plans. The Clery Act (1990) requires colleges and universities to report incidents such as domestic violence, sexual assaults, stalking, etc. in a timely fashion. Title IX (1972) specifically outlines how to handle sexual assault and harassment complaints (Mumper et al., 2016). Incidents investigated by CARE teams result in referrals to a university's counseling services, campus police department, women's resource center, or the Title IX coordinator for resolution (Mahaffie, 2014; Mumper et al., 2016). However, regardless of the particular type of unexpected incident, Clery Act (1990) mandates higher education institutions to compile statistics and disclose campus policies in an annual security report if they participate in federal student financial aid programs (Lipka, 2007; Mahaffie, 2014).

Prior to the 2007 Virginia Tech massacre, all four of the aforementioned legal mandates were in place, but there was a striking lack of coordination among organizational divisions when responding to crises (Lipka, 2007; Virginia Tech Review Panel, 2007). In December 2006, a fellow student raped and murdered Laura Dickinson in her Eastern Michigan University dorm room (Butzel-Long, 2007; U.S. Department of Education, 2007). At the time, senior university officials made an official statement, "no reason to suspect foul play" (Lipka, 2007, p. 2), even as they quietly investigated the situation as a homicide. Approximately two months later, police arrested and charged a student, Orange Amir Taylor III, for Dickinson's murder (Butzel-Long, 2007; U.S. Department of Education, 2007). With the lack of a formal centralized operational safety plan, university officials created a culture of mistrust through their handling, or lack thereof (i.e., attempt to cover up investigative details), that led to the unfortunate situation becoming worse. In failing to notify the campus community in a timely fashion, the university violated the Clery Act, resulting in a record $350,000 fine, a $2.5 million settlement to Dickinson's family and the resignations of three senior-level administrators (U.S. Department of Education, 2007). Furthermore, the U.S. Department of Education's Office of Civil Rights (OCR) directed Eastern Michigan University to appoint a Title IX coordinator to handle sexual assault and harassment complaints, draft new guidelines for resolving such allegations, and allow the OCR to make periodic campus visits to ensure compliance (Jesse, 2010; OCR, 2010).

Four months after the Eastern Michigan University incident, the Virginia Tech community faced what became one of the most horrific massacres to occur on a university campus. In the aftermath of Seung-Hui Cho murdering 32 people and wounding 17 others on April 16, 2007, officials conducted an extensive investigation of the events that led to this tragic event. The VT Review Panel (2007) discovered that some university personnel were aware of Cho's mental health, but provisions of FERPA (1988) and ADA (1990) prohibited them from disclosing information with others. In addition, VT administrators did not have an official operational safety plan in place to handle such a crisis, particularly effective communication with the community that two students had been killed at Ambler Johnston Hall prior to Cho entering Norris Hall two hours later where he continued to kill and wound others (Virginia Tech Review Panel, 2007). This lapse allowed families of two Norris Hall victims to claim a wrongful death lawsuit against the state and university, arguing that a timely warning could have spared their loved ones. Although Montgomery County Circuit Court ruled in favor of the victims' families, the Virginia Supreme Court overturned the ruling, stating that VT officials could not have foreseen additional loss of life (Grasgreen, 2013). Even so, the university eventually paid out approximately $48 million to cover expenses related to this tragedy, which included $100,000 to each victim's family for medical and mental-health expenses (Johnson, 2012; Lipka, 2008).

As a result of this tragedy, Virginia Tech officials took many steps to create a culture of individual and campus preparedness that pervades the community to this day. For example, a number of effective operational safety plans, a concept that did not exist prior to April 16, 2007, now address at multiple organizational levels the legal and logistical challenges associated with risk management, including mitigation and reduction of civil (i.e., tort) liability in a proactive rather than a reactive manner. The Commonwealth of Virginia now mandates that all colleges and universities must develop an operational safety plan (Randazzo & Cameron, 2012; Randazzo & Plummer, 2009; VA Tech Review Panel, 2007). Virginia Tech's institutional culture of individual, department, and university preparedness is further reinforced by it being the first in the nation to earn national accreditation from the Emergency Management Accreditation Program (EMAP) (VT Emergency Management, 2019).

Chapter Three

Selected Institutions

The objective here was to understand the design and implementation process utilized at college-affiliated institutions across the country through the perspectives of five representative organizations. These entities are primarily located in the Commonwealth of Virginia with special attention to coastal regions, which are especially vulnerable to high-stakes natural and manmade disasters (Smith, 2003). Specifically, this region's geography includes the low-lying plains of the Atlantic coast and Chesapeake Bay that are easily inundated by rising tides and overall sea-level rise, which exacerbates the potential for damage from storm surge and tidal flooding (Myers & Lusk, 2017). In addition, the Commonwealth's location along the mid-Atlantic increases the likelihood of a direct hit from a hurricane, tornado, or tropical storm because of global wind patterns, humidity, and air and water temperatures (URI, 2015). Furthermore, with constant turnover in the population resulting from military personnel changes and individuals moving into the area for college or employment, social bonds may be weaker (Braga & Clarke, 2014; Weisburd, Groff, & Yang, 2012). According to Braithwaite (1975), crime exists in densely populated areas where social bonds are weaker, which has been linked to higher urban crime rates. Thus, individuals at college-affiliated institutions in the Commonwealth of Virginia may be vulnerable because "open campuses are as susceptible to violence as any other public place" (Hoover, 2008, p. 707).

At almost two hundred institutions, Virginia's colleges and their affiliates represent a diverse range of missions and institutional characteristics (SCHEV, 2019; VTCHE, 2016). Any one of these organizations could have been selected for examination here, but delegations from four representative institutions (i.e., one university, one college, one research center, and one graduate institution) agreed to participate by offering their operational safety plan documents and insights into their design and implementation process.

An additional institution served as a blue light (i.e., a beacon example representing what an operational safety plan ideally should include to enhance public safety) (BeaconMaster, 2018). The Emergency Management Accreditation Program (EMAP) provides research-based leadership in public safety standards that detail how state and local governments, as well as higher education institutions, are to uphold their stakeholders and communities' "best interests" (EMAP, 2019). However, there are only eight universities in the U.S. that are EMAP accredited (date of original accreditation in parentheses): Virginia Tech University (2014), Idaho State University (2015), University of Alabama (2015), University of Central Florida (2016), Michigan State University (2017), Tufts University (2017), Florida International University (2019), and Washington University (MO) (2020). Personnel at Idaho State University agreed to serve as that blue light institution.

The selection process in obtaining operational safety plans was based on a purposeful sampling method. Criteria for inclusion were based on institutions' unique planning for and responding to sea-level rise, hurricanes, tornadoes, violent crimes (i.e., active shooters), etc. The selected five institutions ". . . show generalizability or diversity . . ." (Bogdan & Biklen, 2007, p.70) in understanding the design and implementation of operational safety plans at college-affiliated institutions across a variety of institutional missions (Creswell, 2013). To provide further context, the following five institutional summaries are offered as a backdrop for understanding the guiding principles, implementation factors, and recommended "best practices" that are presented later in this book.

Preceding chapters of this dissertation provided insight to this study on operational safety plan design and implementation. It was then followed by a comprehensive literature review outlining the theoretical frameworks and research relating to emergency management planning for both natural and manmade events. Lastly, the methodological approach was discussed (i.e., data collection, analysis, and sampling procedures). This multiple case study aimed to identify strategies associated with the design and implementation (i.e., guiding principles, implementation factors, and "best practices") for higher education operational safety plan protocols, a burgeoning area of inquiry. To address this gap in the literature, this comparative case study created a protocol and applied it to the analysis of operational safety plans through the lenses of open systems organizational, rational choice, and chaos theories. Institutions examined included Idaho State University (ISU), Old Dominion University (ODU), Tidewater Community College (TCC), Eastern Virginia Medical School (EVMS), and NASA Langley Research Center.

In this chapter, the investigative results were discovered through a rich description not only from the document analysis, but also the participants' interviews in which the subjects described their institution's operational safety planning process. This investigation was guided by the following research questions: 1) What principles guide the design of operational safety plans for college-affiliated institutions? 2) What factors found within college-affiliated education operational safety plans are critical for successful implementation? 3) What are the "best practices" for operational safety plans that are utilized by college-affiliated institutions?

SUMMARY OF THE INSTITUTIONS' OPERATIONAL SAFETY PLANS

Operational safety plans from Idaho State University, Old Dominion University, Tidewater Community College, Eastern Virginia Medical School, and NASA Langley Research Center yielded evidence in support of all six themes proposed in the document analysis protocol. Using extant research literature as well as local, state, and federal guidelines such as Emergency Management Accreditation Program (EMAP), National Incident Management System (NIMS), and Federal Emergency Management Agency (FEMA), the resulting protocol divided responses to crises and emergencies into: Emergency Management, Resources, Coordination, Communication, Emergency Threat, and Training (Blair & Martaindale, 2013; Barron & Yechiam, 2009; DHS, 2014; EMAP, 2016; FEMA, 2011a; Johnson & Rainey, 2007; Sheldon, 2018; Stafford, 2014). While all six themes were detected in the collected institutional data, the document analysis protocol, and follow-up interview analysis, was sensitive enough to also show significant differences due to unique institutional mission, geographical location, and EMAP certification status.

Chapter Four

Idaho State University

Idaho State University (ISU) is a four-year public institution with a Research III designation that ". . . advances scholarly and creative endeavors through academic instruction, and the creation of new knowledge, research, and artistic works" (ISU, 2018b). This institution is a multi-campus university with sites located in Pocatello, Meridian, and Idaho Falls, with a student population of 12,500 and employs approximately 800 full- and part-time faculty (NCES, 2020). Idaho State University, the second in the nation to obtain the national accreditation from the Emergency Management Accreditation Program (EMAP), maintains a variety of emergency management and action plans, which any community member may access these resources with special permission (ISU, 2020).

As illustrated in figure 4.1, composite data (i.e., document analysis and interview) indicated that Idaho State University (ISU) emphasized Emergency Management (29%) as their main theme.

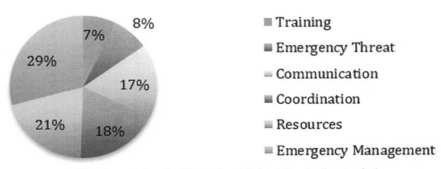

Figure 4.1.   Idaho State University Operational Safety Plan Coding Analysis

ISU's (2019) Emergency Operations Plan, states "The purpose of ISU's EOP is to develop a simple emergency management capability that can take immediate steps to respond to the effects of an emergency, preserve life, protect property, provide assistance, and coordinate the University's continuity of academic and business operations" (p. 9). Numerous examples of the Emergency Management theme were found throughout the plan, such as the following:

> A standardized on-scene emergency management construct specifically designed to provide for the adoption of an integrated organizational structure that reflects the complexity and demands of single or multiple Incidents, without being hindered by jurisdictional boundaries. ICS is the combination of facilities, equipment, personnel, procedures, and communications operating within a common organizational structure, designed to aid in the management of Resources during Incidents. It is used for all kinds of emergencies and applies to small as well as large and complex Incidents. (ISU, 2019, p. 44)

Resources (21%) was ISU's second main theme with its ". . . overall objective . . . to ensure the effective management of emergency efforts involved in preparing for, mitigating against, responding to, and recovering from critical emergencies and disasters" (ISU, 2019, p. 10). Toward that end, ISU (2018a) conducted a *Resource and Emergency Response Gap Analysis* that measured their baseline resource preparedness. ISU Public Safety surveyed operational safety stakeholders and "compared the data generated from the resource list, the response capabilities questionnaire and AAR/IPs to define the gaps" (ISU, 2018a, p. 2). ISU then adjusted their primary Operations Plan to address resource gaps in the following six areas: Geological, Fire, Active Shooter, Bomb/IED/Terrorism, Pandemic/Epidemic, and Cyber/IT. As a result, ISU's

> Operational planning will consider all Threats and Hazards identified in ISU's THIRA and in this EOP to help make informed decisions about how to allocate limited Resources and address safety needs before, during, and after an Incident. ISU's planning objectives, along with an understanding of the required Resources to achieve them and the desired outcomes, will allow ISU's IMT to determine how limited Resources can best be invested to build and sustain capabilities. (ISU, 2019, p. 14)

The third main theme was Coordination (18%) in which ISU's EOP "acts as the fundamental guidance for emergency response on all ISU campuses. The coordination of this EOP and the standard operating procedures within the EOP is an ongoing process through regular training and exercises" (ISU, 2019, p. 2). In fact, the Incident Commander (IC) "in coordination with the with the EOC Manager, will implement the EOP in accordance with the level of emergency based on priorities that include life safety, preservation of property and environment, restoration of essential utilities and functions, and a return to normal operations" (ISU, 2019, p. 13).

Communication (17%) was ISU's fourth main theme. In fact, ISU (2019) Emergency Communications Procedures state that ISU uses ". . . a redundant system of communications capabilities, which include, but are not limited to the following" (p. 35): Radios, Phones, ISU Alerts Emergency Notification System, and Testing and Maintenance Procedures. Furthermore:

> During an [emergency] Incident, ISU will establish a Communications Unit under the Logistics Section. The Communications Unit along with ISU Public Safety Dispatch Center will establish and maintain communications with the President's Executive Policy Group, ISU IMT and ISU First Responders, city dispatchers, and/or the city and county EOCs, as well as other essential external stakeholders or First Responders as deemed necessary. The Communications Unit and Public Safety Dispatch Center will work with the IT/Telecommunications Unit under the Logistics Section to maintain communications on campus. (ISU, 2019, p. 35)

The last two protocol themes came in as follows: Emergency Threat (8%), and Training (7%). In ISU's Continuity of Government Plan (2019), they identified in their 2013 survey six probable threats and hazards to the institution: "Earthquakes, Structural Fires, Bombs/Improvised Explosive Device (IED)/Terrorism, Active Shooter, Pandemic/Epidemic, and Cyber/IT Disruption" (p. 7). On that premise, ISU

> . . . is committed to the safety and protection of its employees, students, operations, and facilities. In support of this commitment, the University has critical operations for continuity of government that must be performed, or rapidly and efficiently resumed in an emergency. The changing threat environment and recent events has raised awareness to the need for continuity of government capabilities that will enable us to continue performance of critical functions across a broad spectrum of emergencies. By planning for operations under such conditions, we hope to mitigate the impact of the incident on our people, our facilities and our mission. (ISU, 2019, p. 5)

Lastly, ISU has established a multi-year training and exercise plan, and its "purpose . . . is to document the University's overall training and exercise program priorities for a specific multi-year time period. These priorities are linked to corresponding core capabilities, and, if applicable, a rationale based on existing strategic guidance, threat assessments, corrective actions from previous exercises, or other factors" (ISU, 2014, p. 19). In addition, "ISU's Department of Public Safety has developed a training and exercise program to support the four (4) mission areas of prepare, mitigate, respond, and re-cover. This program has been designed to help ISU measure the effectiveness of this EOP and to support enhancing internal campus capabilities in both emergency management and Incident response" (ISU, 2019, p. 38).

In summary, Idaho State University (ISU) was selected as a blue light (i.e., a beacon example representing what an operational safety plan should look like for public safety) (BeaconMaster, 2018). To receive EMAP certification, ISU was required to have multiple documents in support of their main opera-tional safety plan (e.g., Hazard Mitigation Plan, Continuity of Government Plan, Resource and Emergency Response Gap Analysis, and eight annexes). According to an ISU representative, the institution uses EMAP guidelines

> . . . because those are the standards. Those are the standards we know of and unless there is a new standard that comes up that shows us something different, that's what we will always go with, but we will always modify things to really meet a higher Ed environment, but that's why we use NIMS and those other benchmarks for writing our plans . . . [as well as] . . . team training on how to develop high quality emergency operations plan . . .

These attributes of ISU's operational safety plan distinguished it from the fol-lowing four non-EMAP certified institutions examined in this study.

Chapter Five

Old Dominion University

Old Dominion University (ODU) is a four-year public institution with a Research II designation that offers academic programs, facilitates strategic partnerships, and engages in active civic commitment with members of the Commonwealth and the nation (ODU, 2018c). The institution's main campus is located in Norfolk, VA, with a student population of approximately 24,000 and employing about 1,500 full- and part-time faculty (NCES, 2020). The Office of Emergency Management (OEM) maintains the institution's Crisis and Emergency Management Plan (CEMP), and any ODU community member with a Monarch Identification and Authorization System (MIDAS) login credential can access its basic plan (ODU, 2018b). Of special note, the ODU Resilience Collaborative conducts research into sea-level rise and climate change, results of which are incorporated into the institution's operational safety plans (Myers & Lusk, 2017; ODU, 2018e).

As illustrated in figure 5.1, composite data (i.e., document analysis and interview) indicated that Old Dominion University (ODU) emphasized Emergency Management (31%) as their main theme.

Figure 5.1.   Old Dominion University Operational Safety Plan Coding Analysis

Old Dominion University's (ODU) operational safety plan (i.e., Crisis and Emergency Management Plan [CEMP]) Promulgation Statement states it:

> . . . is a multidisciplinary, all-hazards plan that establishes a comprehensive framework for the management of incidents, emergencies, and events at any ODU campus in the Hampton Roads, Virginia region. The plan is implemented when it becomes necessary to mobilize the resources of the identified departments and agencies to save lives, protect property and infrastructure, preserve mission continuity, and return to a state of normalcy. The plan assigns major roles and responsibilities to departments and agencies and requires annual planning, training, and exercising prior to a real world event to respond effectively. This plan represents a commitment by University leadership to work together to prevent, mitigate against, prepare for, respond to, and recover from emergencies in our community. (ODU, 2019, p. 1)

ODU is guided by the provision in the Code of Virginia 23.1-804, which states:

> The governing board of each public institution of higher education shall develop, adopt, and keep current a written crisis and emergency management plan. The plan shall . . . require the Department of Criminal Justice Services and the Virginia Criminal Injuries Compensation Fund to be contacted immediately to deploy assistance in the event of an emergency as defined in the emergency response plan. . . . Every four years, each public institution of higher education shall conduct a comprehensive review and revision of its crisis and emergency management plan to ensure that the plan remains current, and the revised plan shall be adopted formally by the governing board. Such review shall also be certified in writing to the Department of Emergency Management. The institution shall coordinate with the local emergency management organization, as defined in § 44-146.16, to ensure integration into the local emergency operations plan . . . higher education shall annually conduct a test or exercise in accordance with the protocols established by the institution's crisis and emergency management plan and certify in writing to the Department of Emergency Management that such a test or exercise was conducted.

In order to comply with this state mandate, ODU emergency managers address hazard situations by "using best practice guidance from Federal, State, and local sources and the higher education sector . . . for incidents, emergencies, and events at ODU" (ODU, 2019, p. 13). Furthermore, ODU's CEMP is designed using a framework whose objectives are to "prevent, mitigate against, prepare for, respond to, and recover from emergencies . . ." (ODU, 2019, p. 1, 13, 15, 21)

As shown in the reprinted schematic (figure 5.2) from the university's CEMP, ODU's Emergency Management Cycle Framework begins with Prevention and Mitigation, which are designed to prevent and mitigate risks to

Figure 5.2. Old Dominion University's Emergency Management Cycle

individuals and property from known threats (ODU, 2019). In the Preparedness section, ODU educates the public on hazard strategies as well as providing training and exercises to the campus community (ODU, 2019). Response
strategies are designed for short-term incidents, with the objective of preventing loss of life, property, and the environment (ODU, 2019). Lastly, there is
no well-defined line between Response and Recovery; however, during these
phases, the ODU management team will coordinate with Federal and State
entities for assistance as needed (ODU, 2019).

For ODU's emergency management planning, the team categorized known
threats that are more likely to occur at the various ODU campus locations
(active threat, bomb/explosion, civil unrest/demonstration, Code Adam, data
breach, earthquake, extreme temperature, flooding, etc.) (ODU, 2019). There
are eighteen annexes that provide guidance when implementing responses to
each known emergency, beginning with a purpose description, scope of the
issue, describing the potential situation, specifying planning assumptions,
concepts of the operations, and providing roles and responsibilities during the
emergency (ODU, 2019). Unlike Idaho State University's (2018a) formal *Resource and Emergency Response Gap Analysis* document, it was unclear how

ODU identified their specific list of eighteen emergency threats for which to develop response annexes.

Resources (22%) was the second major theme under which ". . . University staff and select other personnel work collaboratively to define emergency priorities, . . . assign resources, and coordinate requests for assistance" (ODU, 2019, p. 25). In fact, "Resources may be shifted, for example, to higher priority incidents . . . [or they] . . . may also be acquired from outside the affected area" (ODU, 2019, p. 26). Should the emergency overwhelm campus resources, ODU follows procedures similar to what was observed for the other higher education institutions examined in this study; that is, the university's senior emergency management leadership will submit a formal request for additional resources to local or county Emergency Managers/Coordinators. For example, the Norfolk City Emergency Management Coordinator can request resources for ODU while the Commonwealth of Virginia Governor's Office will coordinate resources for all incidents and critical events (ODU, 2019). If needed, ODU can also request federal resources as well as those from the private sector, which ". . . include large, medium, and small businesses; commerce, private cultural and educational institutions; and industry, as well as public/private partnerships that have been established specifically for emergency management purposes" (ODU, 2019, p. 46).

The third major theme was Coordination (19%). According to an ODU representative, emergency management personnel views Coordination as follows:

> . . . we do all . . . plan development, coordination in terms of assembling subject matter experts, functional area level representatives, and essentially putting a team of people that will annually look at different components of the plan soliciting their feedback capturing it and putting that into one large document that ultimately coordinating by my office and pushed up the ladder to . . . ultimately the President . . .

ODU's basic CEMP plan ". . . includes critical information pertaining to organizational structures, roles and responsibilities, command/control/*coordination*, and other strategic-level operational concerns . . . in a coordinated manner to provide for the health, safety, security, and mission continuity of the institution" (ODU, 2019, pp. 14–15).

The fourth major theme is Communication (14%). In ODU's emergency plan, it states that, "The CEMP is modeled in accordance with best practices in the emergency management field, including incorporation of the National Incident Management System (NIMS) to facilitate . . . communication between all responding entities" (ODU, 2019, p. 16). In planning for an incident or critical event, "There may be . . . widespread . . . communications outages [that] may require the use of alternate methods of providing public information and delivering essential services" (ODU, 2019, p. 22). Also,

Natural	Technological	Human-Caused
Earthquake	Data and System Breach	Active Threat
Extreme Temperature	Hazardous Materials Spill/ Release	Bomb Threat/Explosion
Flooding (pluvial, tidal, and storm surge)	Infrastructure Failure	Civil Unrest/Demonstration
Hurricane/Tropical Storm/ Nor'easter	Structure Fire/Arson	Code Adam/Missing Child
Lightning		Medical Emergency
Severe Weather/Tornado		Public Health Incident
Winter Storm		Threat of Harm/Criminal Activity

Figure 5.3.   Old Dominion University's Threats and Hazards

"Communications may be problematic due to demands exceeding capacities [, but] protection and restoration of critical infrastructure and key resources is a priority" (ODU, 2019, p. 22).

Lastly, Emergency Threat (8%) and Training (6%) were relatively minor themes in ODU's CEMP plan. ODU categorizes ". . . a wide spectrum of threats and hazards . . . all of which have the potential to disrupt University operations, cause damage, and create casualties" (ODU, 2019, p. 19) as reprinted from the CEMP (figure 5.3).

A salient Human-Caused threat to the University and campus community is "Myriad public health threats (e.g., Zika virus, MRSA, norovirus, tuberculosis, influenza, meningitis, and other communicable diseases, etc.) [that] have the potential to spread quickly throughout campus, especially among the resident student population" (ODU, 2019, p. 20). During an interview with an ODU representative,

> . . . Covid [-19] is a prime example . . . we did not have a formal extension plan of the Crisis Emergency Management Plan that specifically talked about pandemic outbreak response . . . but there is a plan that already exists with student health services that relates to pandemic outbreak response. So essentially we kind of piggybacked off that one used . . .

In summary, Old Dominion University's CEMP plan was 451 pages with eighteen annexes all combined into one comprehensive document. Even though ODU's CEMP plan was not EMAP certified, the emergency management team relied on EMAP, NIMS, FEMA, etc. for guidance. When asked about the plan's thoroughness despite no EMAP accreditation, an ODU representative replied, "If you go to EMAP online.org and look at the standard of the 64 elements . . . there is a lot of work for us to be able to be assessment ready. We have a lot that needs to be done. We have some plans that have not been developed yet." Finally, ODU was the only institution in the Hampton Roads region included in this study whose operational safety plan discussed sea-level rise as a threat.

Chapter Six

Tidewater Community College

Tidewater Community College (TCC) is a two-year public institution with a High Transfer-Mixed Traditional/Nontraditional Carnegie Classification. TCC's mission is to provide education and training to all individuals of the Commonwealth to support them in reaching their individual goals while contributing to the diverse global community (TCC, 2018a). The institution operates four campuses located in the Virginia Beach, Norfolk, Portsmouth, and Chesapeake cities with an undergraduate enrollment of approximately 23,000 and employing about 1,200 full- and part-time faculty members (NCES, 2020). The Director of Public Safety maintains the institution's Crisis and Emergency Management Plan (CEMP), and any TCC community member can access basic emergency preparedness information from the college's website. However, only certain individuals can have full access to the college's official CEMP on a need-to-know basis (TCC, 2018b). During a potential shooting in the summer of 2017, where a male student brandished a firearm at a female professor, communication was less than optimal between senior leaders, security personnel, and the Virginia Beach Police Department (Satchell, 2017). This incident prompted the update of TCC's operational safety plan (Baumgarten, personal communication, 2017).

As illustrated in figure 6.1, composite data (i.e., document analysis and interview) indicates that Tidewater Community College (TCC) emphasized Emergency Management (29%) as their main theme.

Tidewater Community College (TCC)'s Crisis and Emergency Management Plan (CEMP) was authorized and approved by the State Board of Community Colleges (VCCS). During a TCC interview, a representative stated, "The State Board for Community Colleges oversee[s] the VCCS. The Chancellor answers to the SBCC. The members of the SBCC are appointed by the Governor" (TCC, 2020). The Plan is designed to respond to emergencies and disasters "in order to save lives; to protect public health, safety, and property;

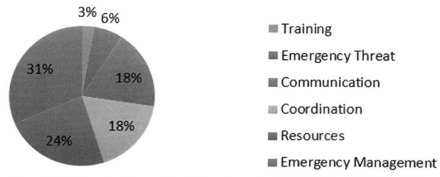

3% 6%

31%

18%

18%

24%

■ Training

■ Emergency Threat

■ Communication

■ Coordination

■ Resources

■ Emergency Management

Figure 6.1. Tidewater Community College Operational Safety Plan Coding Analysis

to restore essential services; and to enable and assist with economic recovery (TCC, 2017, p. v). Furthermore, TCC is "vulnerable to myriad natural hazards, including hurricanes, floods, winter storms, and other severe weather. TCC is also vulnerable to technological incidents such as power outages, hazardous materials events, and manmade disasters such as terrorism and violent crimes and cyber security incident" (TCC, 2017, p. xiii). TCC has identified twelve threats for which annexes were created with specific instructions on how personnel will respond to any of those incidents.

The premise of TCC's basic Crisis and Emergency Management Plan (CEMP) is to prepare, respond, recover, and mitigate action in the event of an emergency or crisis situation (TCC, 2017). "Each campus operates independently under the authority and responsibility of the Campus Provost and relies on college-wide resources provided by the college's District Administration offices" (TCC, 2017, p. 5). However, effective July 1, 2020, TCC eliminated all Campus Provost positions, and, according to a TCC representative, "Each campus is now managed by a Campus Dean. The CEMP will need to be updated to reflect this" (TCC, 2020). At the same time, members of the district office instruct faculty to insert the following in their course syllabus for emergency preparedness, something that was not seen with the four-year institutions or affiliates:

In the event of a bomb threat, tornado, or fire, students and staff may be directed to evacuate the building or move to an internal assembly area location within the building. Evacuation routes are posted in each classroom. The map indicates the route to the nearest exit. Students should review the map to make sure that the exit routes for the building area are clearly understood. The information regarding locations of the Emergency Assembly Areas and Internal Assembly Areas for all classrooms or spaces used on the various campuses is available at the following link: http//web.tcc.edu/emergency/cemp.htm. If you will require assistance during an evacuation, let your instructor know at the end of the first class. (TCC, 2017, p. E-1-6)

Lastly, TCC security personnel (Top Guard) is structured to triage the emergency crisis, call the first responders (i.e., local police, fire, etc.), and then turn command over to the first responders upon arrival. In fact, during the interview with a TCC representative, it was shared that, "One legal factor is we have . . . contract security and they are hands off. They . . . have no stopping or arrest powers so we have to write our response to certain crises knowing that all we can do is sit back and wait for the police to arrive." The representative continued:

Which has led to the reality that we need to commission a police force and have our own independent TCC police force, and we are heavily involved in that right now I have a meeting this afternoon for another follow-up. We are getting ready to the new president commissioned a committee to study this and meet with stakeholders around the college and discuss it and kind of interview students and faculty and get their feedback and what it would be like to have an armed police force on campus, but we're definitely moving that way.

The second main theme is Resources (24%). In TCC's CEMP plan, it "assigns roles and responsibilities to campus/district administration positions, divisions and departments or, in some cases, to specific positions that are directly responsible for emergency response and critical support services and that provide a management structure for . . . deploying essential resources" (TCC, 2017, p. 1). In addition:

Disasters affecting TCC may affect the surrounding community. Therefore, it is necessary for TCC to prepare for and carry out disaster response and short-term recovery operations in conjunction with local resources, such as police, fire, and emergency medical services responders. As a matter of state policy, institutions of higher education (IHE) are required to coordinate resources and requests for assistance through the local emergency management agency. (TCC, 2017, p. 5)

Resource assistance is also allocated through state, federal, private, and volunteer organizations as well as adjoining jurisdictional agencies.

Coordination (18%) is the third main theme highlighted in the analysis of TCC's CEMP plan. In TCC's Promulgation Statement (see figure 6.2), it states that the Director of Public Safety is the college's Emergency Coordination Officer (ECO) and, as alternates, the Director of Facilities and The Dean of Health Professions will assume the role (TCC, 2017).

Emergency Management Coordinator's Succession Order	
Primary	Director of Public Safety
Alternate #1	Director of Facilities
Alternate #2	Dean of Health Professions
Alternate #3	Security Manager

Figure 6.2.   TCC Emergency Management Coordinator's Succession Order

TCC is guided by the Virginia Department of Emergency Management (VDEM) outline, which utilizes concepts from the National Incident Management System (NIMS). This allows TCC the ability to coordinate with local jurisdictions (i.e., internal and external emergency agencies on the local, state, and federal level) (TCC, 2017).

Implementation of the CEMP requires extensive cooperation, collaboration, and information sharing across all college campuses and departments as well as with local, state, and federal entities. "Use of this plan enables the college to operate seamlessly in disaster conditions and to provide a safe and secure environment for the TCC community . . . two other college documents support TCC's ability to respond to and recover from an emergency: Continuity of Operations (COOP) Plan . . . [and] . . . IT Contingency Planning and Business Recovery Plan" (TCC, 2017, p. xiii).

TCC also utilizes the Incident Command System (ICS) to coordinate efforts with their departments and agencies in order to "work toward the common goal of stabilizing an incident and protecting life, property, and the environment (TCC, 2017, p. 8).

Communication (18%) also came in third as a main theme highlighted in the analysis. TCC created an Emergency Policy Group (EPG) that recommends policy and communications during a major emergency to the College President. The Incident Management Team (IMT) duties include communicating during an incident, and making decisions and recommendations for evacuation, campus closings, the campus community, and notifications of shelter-in-place (TCC, 2017, p. 19). TCC's Emergency Operations Center (EOC) also "is where all resources information are routed during a disaster situation and is activated by the President or Emergency Management Coordinator. Individuals in the TCC EOC collect, coordinate, and disseminate the information and communications necessary to deal with a disaster situation" (TCC, 2017, pp. 30–31).

Lastly, Emergency Threat (6%) and Training (3%) themes were identified in TCC's CEMP plan. A TCC representative stated that they ". . . inherited what is in there" (TCC, 2020) (i.e., the list of threats identified), and consequently created twelve annexes with specific instructions on how to respond to a particular emergency's risks and impacts. TCC's (2017) "Director of Public Safety, through the executive staff, is responsible for the development, maintenance, testing, and exercising of this CEMP" (p. 46). In fact, these senior administrators as part of the Incident Management Team (IMT)

> . . . meets periodically throughout the year to improve preparedness measures through training and participating in emergency drills or exercises. The IMT participates in reviewing, writing, and updating plans and procedures, including this CEMP. The campus provost ensures staff are trained on emergency procedures and provides staff members with written plans and checklists for references. (TCC, 2017, p. 27)

In summary, what makes TCC's CEMP unique is that they do not have a dedicated police force to keep the college safe. To reiterate, the TCC representative stated that they are ". . . contract security and they are hands off. They . . . have no stopping or arrest powers . . .," which is why they are currently in the process of creating a certified police force. As of now, in an event of any disaster, TCC personnel has to wait for local authorities to arrive, which is why they rely on their faculty, staff, and students (i.e., if they see something, say something). In fact, TCC's executive leadership mandates that faculty insert emergency instructions in their syllabi. TCC, like many other community colleges, relies on their faculty to provide support service functions beyond instruction due to limited financial resources that limit student services relative to what is typically found at four-year institutions (Cohen, Brawer, & Kisker, 2014). Therefore, TCC faculty members also serve as de facto members of the college's emergency management team by assisting with directing students on what to do during a crisis event.

Chapter Seven

Eastern Virginia Medical School

Eastern Virginia Medical School (EVMS) is a four-year public graduate and research teaching institution for the health sciences located in Norfolk, VA. EVMS' mission as an academic facility for professionals is to achieve excellence in medical and health education, research, and patient care (EVMS, 2018a). The medical school supports 1,300 graduate students and approximately 400 full- and part-time faculty (NCES, 2020). The Vice President for Administration and Finance and Emergency Manager is responsible for the School's Emergency Operations Plan (EOP). This emergency plan is readily accessible to the public or any interested parties via EVMS' website (EVMS, 2018b). The U.S. Department of Health and Human Services provides guidelines recognizing that medical facilities such as EVMS present unique challenges when it comes to designing and implementing operational safety plans (USHHS-OIG, 2019). That is, EVMS emergency management personnel must account for the safety of students, faculty, staff, patients, visitors, and research animal subjects during natural and manmade crises (EVMS, 2019).

As illustrated in figure 7.1, composite data (i.e., document analysis and interview) indicated that Eastern Virginia Medical School (EVMS) emphasized Emergency Management (27%) as their main theme.

In EVMS's Operational Safety Plan, it states its purpose ". . . is to establish a comprehensive, all hazards approach to managing disasters and emergencies at EVMS across a spectrum of activities including mitigation, preparedness, response, and recovery" (EVMS, 2017, p. 1). Furthermore, the ". . . plan is designed to address natural and human-caused hazards that could adversely affect the school. It covers the full range of complex and constantly changing requirements in anticipation of or in response to threats of or actual disasters and emergency" (EVMS, 2017, p. 1). EMVS models its plans from the National Response Framework (NRF) and the National Incident Management System (NIMS) as well as with the Virginia Department of Emergency Man-

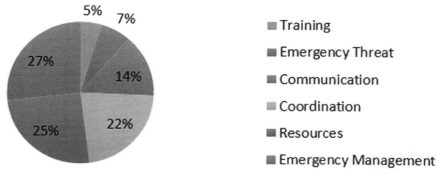

Figure 7.1.   Eastern Virginia Medical School Operational Safety Plan Coding Analysis

agement guidelines and development for higher education. EOP management also collaborates with local, state, and federal emergency agencies in designing and implementing the plan during an emergency (EVMS, 2017). EVMS (2017) EOC personnel will also ". . . monitor, coordinate, task, demobilize, and recover EVMS resources in support of resolving the emergency" (p. 35). An EVMS representative shared that their EOC plan is reviewed annually:

> . . . to see how things work, what needs to be improved, and also we monitor any changes Virginia Department of Emergency Management anytime they make recommendations for changes or changes in the law or you know best practices we would also look at our review and update. We are also constantly in flux here in terms of personnel as far as buildings, where classes are held, how they are held, and on our clinical side, how they handle things, what have you so we're constantly reviewing it by constantly we review it as changes occur. But we do at least an annual review and then of course we follow the guidelines of the Virginia Department of Emergency Management for doing updates and submitting those to the vice president of administration and finance to submit to the board for final approval. (EVMS, 2020)

Resources (25%) is the second highest theme, and as such "The EVMS EOC will be staffed and operated as the situation dictates. When activated, operations will be supported by representatives from EVMS departments who will provide information, data, resources, and recommendations regarding actions needed to cope with emergency and disaster situations" (EVMS, 2017, p. 5). "Upon receiving information about the specifics of the incident, the EVMS Incident Commander will activate the appropriate functional annexes, as needed, to mobilize assets and the deployment of resources to support the incident" (EVMS, 2017, p. 19). According to EVMS's Emergency Operations Plan,

Emergency Resources and supplies will be procured by the Finance and Administration Section in coordination with the Logistics Section, according to EVMS emergency procurement procedures. Acquisition, distribution, and demobilization of resources will be conducted in a manner consistent with existing EVMS policies, ICS/NIMS guidelines, and legal requirements. (EVMS, 2017, p. 19)

EVMS EOP Base Plan has annexes and appendices that outline how to respond to and meet the demands of a disaster. EVMS (2017) "Emergency Operations Plans identify the available personnel, equipment, facilities, supplies, and other resources and state the method or scheme for coordinated actions to be taken by individuals and government services in the event of natural and man-made disasters" (p. 119).

EVMS's EOP managers created an annex, Agriculture and Natural Resources, that ". . . establishes actions EVMS departments must take in support of coordinating and executing emergency management activities that encompass securing and caring for research assets and animal research subjects, as emergency events dictate" (p. 72), language that is not explicitly found in other university-wide emergency operational safety plans (e.g., ISU, ODU, and TCC). In fact, EVMS gives specific instructions on how to care for animals in the event of an emergency, such as a power outage, loss of water, or a hurricane. In the event there is a water loss, for example, "Rabbits can get iceberg lettuce, apples, or pineapples. Guinea pigs can get fruit as well. Any animal experiencing dehydration can be given subcutaneous fluids or gavaged water orally" (EVMS, 2017, p. 76). The care instructions are to ensure that employees responsible for the research animals during an emergency are in compliance with the Institutional Animal Care and Use Committee (IACUC) protocols (USDA, 2020). Regardless of institutional efforts, a crisis has the potential to significantly disrupt animal research in progress anyway and, therefore, "The ERG [Emergency Response Group] will work with researchers to recover and/or replace any lost research to the extent possible" (EVMS, 2017, p. 77).

The third main theme was identified as Coordination (22%) in which the EVMS (2017) Emergency Management personnel "coordinates the activities of, and supports all departments and partner organizations across the spectrum of emergency management. Activities include alert and notification, staffing or staff augmentation, deployment of emergency response teams, incident action planning, coordination of operations, logistics and materiel, direction and control, and information management" (p. 7). The EOP provides a framework for coordinating with local hospitals, public health and medical services, search and rescue teams as well as responding alongside external emergency services related to all hazardous responses (EVMS, 2017). The Emergency Response Group (ERG) is led by the Vice President of Administration & Finance (EVMS Incident Commander) and will coordinate all critical resource management necessary to control the emergency or disaster. This will consist of collecting and evaluating information from on scene incident command, emergency responders and EVMS departments, and coordinating the response with support agencies, local officials, and other tenants of the Eastern Virginia Medical Center, i.e., Sentara Norfolk General Hospital (SNGH), Children's Hospital of the King's Daughters (CHKD), City of Norfolk Public Health, and private businesses. The ERG will direct the deployment of EVMS resources and adjust the emergency response based on information received from on-scene responders. The ERG ensures continuity of basic school services and operations during protracted incidents that require a campus-wide response. The EVMS Incident Commander seeks out the support, guidance, and advice of the ERG members in planning for and responding to disaster situations. The ERG is composed of school officials who will take operational actions necessary to support a disaster response. Some ERG members will staff the EOC for the duration of the disaster and will route communications through the EOC and make critical operational decisions as the situation warrants (EVMS, 2017, p. 10).

Communication (14%) was EVMS's fourth main theme as exemplified by an appendix, *Emergency Notification and Crisis Communication*, in which "EVMS EOP establishes actions EVMS departments must take in support of coordinating and executing emergency management activities that encompass disseminating information regarding an emergency event to the onsite campus population and to external recipients, as emergency events dictate" (p. 103). In fact, this appendix identifies actions for when to activate, when to respond and recover, and when to communicate information throughout an emergency. The appendix also facilitates situational awareness and prioritizes information resources requests to external support services (EVMS, 2017).

According to the EVMS (2017) EOP:

> Marketing and Communications is the primary department for coordinating with other EVMS departments and external agencies providing Emergency Notification and Crisis Communications resources. During an urgent event requiring immediate life safety information to be distributed to the campus community, EVMS Police and Public Safety will take the lead. Other EVMS departments may assist in emergency notification and crisis communications efforts as well. (p. 104)

Communication can sometimes present problems. For example, an EVMS representative shared:

> . . . about seven years ago we had a scenario where we had State Police, Norfolk Police quite of few people participated in an active shooter event, after that we

found out that 1) as usual in any event communications when you have multiple agencies became a problem. We have since been able to add on our radios a talk around channel so we can communicate with various responding agencies on that system so that was one thing that we recognized that we had to do because before we had old 800 MH radio system and ours were analog and everyone else gone digital we finally gone to digital and be able to add additional channels. We also added radio communications to our housekeeping people, our facility people and our environmental health and safety people so that during these crises we had radio communications direct with them as well because we recognized there were shortcomings there so there . . . that was the main thing that we were able to do as far as looking at something and say where did this go wrong. (EVMS, 2020)

The last two protocol themes for EVMS were Emergency Threat (7%) and Training (5%). EVMS (2017) identified fourteen hazards in their Hazard Vulnerability Assessment that have the potential to disrupt the college community. EVMS (2017) EOP states: "During a threat of a disaster or actual disaster, or an evacuation, all departments that are assigned primary and supporting responsibilities in Annexes to this EOP will maintain on-going communication and coordinate media releases with the Public Information Officer in the EVMS EOC" (p. 5). In addition, EOC personnel will conduct an ". . . initial assessment [which] will focus on life threatening damage and major destruction to the exterior of buildings. Priority for assessments will be given to buildings and infrastructure serving the following functions: buildings housing technology equipment, campus utilities, animal research facilities, patient care facilities, and parking garages" (p. 20). Meanwhile, with regards to Training, the EVMS EOP states that:

> The Emergency Manager, in cooperation with EVMS Executive Leadership, will conduct annual training and exercises to ensure that EVMS staff and their respective departments are familiar with this EOP and their roles in an emergency response. The exercises and training will be part of EVMS' multi-year training and exercise plan . . . (EVMS, 2017, p. 22)

Furthermore, the Emergency Manager will coordinate and track individuals' training records to ensure they are NIMS compliant; they will also create improvement plans and after action reports to improve and update the operational safety plan (EVMS, 2017).

In summary, the Eastern Virginia Medical School (EVMS) is a graduate, medical, and research institution, which was included because it affords a different perspective on operational safety plan design, implementation, and best practices. The main EVMS campus in the City of Norfolk is in close proximity to Sentara Norfolk General Hospital, Children's Hospital of the King's

Daughters (CHKD), and the City's Public Health Department because this arrangement facilitates medical professionals' education (i.e., complete their degrees and clinical requirements) all in one location. EVMS's EOP is unique because it provides guidelines to protect both academic and medical assets (e.g., patients, medical equipment, research animals, etc.). For example, the EVMS EOP specifically provides how much water, fruits, or lettuce must be given to rabbits and guinea pigs during power outages, loss of water, or hurricanes. This kind of verbiage is not observed in the operational safety plans at the other studied institutions. An emphasis on protecting research assets, in addition to the academic stakeholders, in EVMS's EOP reflects the higher importance placed on research endeavors by graduate institutions.

Chapter Eight

NASA Langley Research Center (NASA LaRC)

NASA Langley Research Center (NASA LaRC) is a collection of nearly two hundred facilities that support aeronautical, Earth science, and space technology research. Situated on 764 acres in Hampton, VA, NASA's oldest field center employs approximately 3,400 individuals who frequently collaborate with local industries and higher education institutions throughout the Commonwealth and our nation (NASA LaRC, 2018a). NASA's missions and values are to safely advance knowledge, education, innovation, and economic vitality in the areas of science, technology, aeronautics, and peaceful exploration of space (NASA LaRC, 2018b). Emergency Operations Center Management, within the Safety and Mission Assurance Branch, is responsible for creating the Center's Emergency Management Plan (EMP), which employees can only view while on-center behind NASA's IT security firewall (Sensitive But Unclassified [SBU]). Although Center personnel can access NASA's EMP, certain other supporting documents are classified and can only be viewed by emergency personnel on a need-to-know basis (NASA LaRC, 2018c). NASA contributes to the world's understanding of climate change through its research programs (NASA JPL, 2019). In fact, these understandings inform operational safety planning at all 10 NASA Field Centers across the country.

As illustrated in figure 8.1, composite data (i.e., document analysis and interview) indicates that NASA Langley Research Center emphasized Emergency Management (35%) as their main theme.

The premise of NASA Langley Research (LaRC) Center (2015) Emergency Management Plan (EMP) is that it:

> establishes uniform policy and guidelines for the effective mitigation of, preparation for, response to, and recovery from a variety of emergency situations. These emergency situations, created by natural and technological hazards, could have a varying degree of impact on the health, safety, and welfare of employees

and visitors to National Aeronautics and Space Administration (NASA) LaRC. To ensure continuity of operations, the application of the provisions for the EMP will be executed by responding organizations through the National Incident Management System (NIMS). (p. 79)

NASA (2015) stated that "NIMS will be the standard on-scene, all-hazards incident management system for firefighters, hazardous materials teams, rescuers, security, and emergency medical teams" (p. 7). The reasoning, according to NASA (2015), is that NIMS incorporates "existing best practices" in keeping with the nationwide management approach to all potential hazards" (p. 7). NASA (2015) basic plan outlines the possible situations that may jeopardize LaRC's operations, which are "technological emergencies, natural disasters, or terrorist attacks" (p. 10). In addition, emergency "management officials, supervisors, and leads will ensure their employees are familiar with the EMP and know their supporting roles and responsibilities" (NASA, 2015, p. 17). NASA's EMP is considered sensitive but unclassified and is valid for five years before it expires. Lastly, Emergency Management Elements are as follow:

Mitigation: Deals with any activities that prevent an emergency, reduce the chance of an emergency happening, or reduce the damaging effects of unavoidable emergencies. *Preparedness*: Includes developing plans for what to do, where to go, or who to call for help before an event occurs. *Response*: Personnel who are involved in responding to and controlling an emergency. *Recovery*: Includes actions taken to return to normal operations following an emergency. (NASA, 2015, p. 29)

Resources (21%) is the second highest theme in NASA's EMP plan. Moreover, NASA (2015) states, "during an emergency operation, certain functions

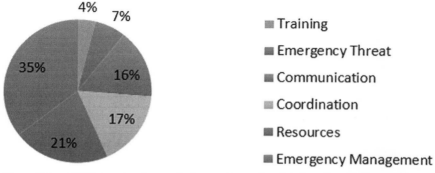

Figure 8.1.   NASA Langley Research Center Operational Safety Plan Coding Analysis

must be assigned and carried out to make the management of the emergency a success. The appropriate lead functions, both Government and contractor will ensure that the actions listed in each Langley Procedural Requirement (LPR) are planned for and that resources are available during an emergency" (p. 17). All NASA resources may be used during large-scale emergencies in order to ensure proper preparation, sustainability, and to recover from the event (NASA, 2015). According to NASA's (2015) EMP, resources will be used based on the extent of emergency and will be categorized by three levels:

> Level I: A situation is in progress or has occurred which is beyond the day-to-day emergency incident, but is confined to a small area or population and does not appear to pose a continuing threat to life or property or to be beyond the capabilities of the emergency responders and security services.

> Level II: A situation is in progress or has occurred which is a special emergency incident, involving a large area or population, which poses a continuing threat to life or property and may require protective actions or additional resources beyond the capabilities of the responding Local Fire department and\ or security officers.

> Level III: A situation is in progress or has occurred, involving a large area/ population, which has caused significant human or economic loss and continues to pose an immediate threat that requires protective actions and additional resources. (NASA, 2015, p. 29)

Coordination (17%) is the third highest theme identified in NASA's EMP plan.

NASA LaRC Emergency Managers are responsible for "coordinating the response and recovery activities for a major emergency/disaster at LaRC, even though the Center's resources may be exhausted. Coordination of Emergency response activities between local, state, and federal levels of government can generally best be accomplished from a single location or the EOC" (NASA, 2015, p. 33). In addition, "The EOC Team has the responsibility for coordination and liaison with city, county, state and federal officials in dealing with an immediate response or recovery for a major emergency, including media relations and public information" (NASA, 2015, p. 36). When an incident does occur,

> On-scene coordination during the incident response phase will be handled by the Senior Fire Officer (SFO) or IC. The EM will provide the necessary coordination between the SFO or IC and LaRC management. The EOC will be opened as directed by the EM. The decision to open the EOC will be determined on a case-by-case basis. Once activated, the EOC will be the coordination point for all activities not associated with on-scene emergency response. All activities during the recovery phase will be coordinated by the Damage Assessment and

Recovery Team. This team will be appointed by the EM, SFO/IC, and the Center
Director. (NASA, 2015, p. 76)

Communication (16%) was NASA's fourth main theme. Once an emergency arises, the Emergency Operations Center (EOC) "will establish communications with the Incident Commander (IC) or the Unified Command
(UC) and will be the main location for coordination of information and
resources" (NASA, 2015, p. 7). Also, "the Office of Strategic Analysis,
Communications and Business Development (OSACB), News Media Team
(NMT), and Public Affairs (PA) are vital part of the EOC, providing media
support, coordination, and dissemination of official news and information"
(NASA, 2015, p. 7). NASA (2015) EOC communication and information
sharing function ". . . is to coordinate the flow of communications between
the different agencies, different levels of government and the public . . ."
(p. 37). In fact, NASA (2015)

> . . . EOC is equipped with cell and landline telephones, additionally; the EOC
> has an Operational Intercommunication System (OIS), Amateur HAM Radio,
> Telecommunications Shared Resources (SHARES) High Frequency Radio,
> satellite radio/telephone, 400/800 MHz, City-wide radios. To support secure
> communications, the Secure Telephone Equipment (STE-III) is available and
> online in the EOC. (p. 10)

Strict communication guidelines govern the release of information at NASA,
stipulating several conditions that an employee must follow. For example,
NASA's Public Affairs Office personnel provide control of release of information through fact sheets, status reports, advisories, notes to editors,
news conferences, news releases, and responses to queries (NASA, 2015).
Employees must refer outside media to these official documents or restate
the information found in those releases. Any requests for information beyond
official news sources must be referred to Public Affairs.

The last two protocol themes were Emergency Threat (7%) and Training
(4%). NASA (2015) created a Hazard/Threat Vulnerability Analysis, and like
the universities and community college in this study, NASA too is susceptible
to natural, technological, and manmade disasters. NASA (2015) states that by
having "knowledge of these hazards, their frequency, and our vulnerability to
them allow LaRC to better assess the risk, to plan, and prepare for the consequences" (p. 22). In fact, NASA (2015) defines a major threat/disaster as:

> . . . Any natural catastrophe (including, without limitation, hurricane, tor-
> nado, storm, flood, high water, wind driven water, tidal water, snowstorm, or
> drought) or, regardless of cause, any fire, flood, or explosion, in any part of
> the United States or its territories which, in the determination of the Presi-

dent, causes damage of sufficient severity and magnitude to warrant assistance under Title 42, United States Code, Sections 5121–5204, to supplement the efforts and available resources of States, local governments, and disaster relief organizations in alleviating the damage, loss, hardship, or suffering caused thereby. (p. 29)

In NASA's (2015) Basic Emergency Management Plan, it states its mission is "to mitigate the effects of known threats, prepare viable plans and procedures to save lives and protect high value resources, to respond with capable emergency response forces during emergencies, and to coordinate an effective recovery system to return to normal operations after natural and technological emergencies and disasters" (p. 10).

Lastly, NASA (2015), under the guidelines of NIMS as it relates to training, states that "preparedness is implemented through a continuous cycle of planning, training, equipping, exercising, evaluating, and taking action to correct and mitigate" (p. 7). In addition, ". . . LaRC Emergency Manager (EM) will conduct exercises to evaluate the planning and training of the emergency response forces. The LaRC EM will coordinate the training, scheduling, and conduct of integrated emergency preparedness exercises with LAFB, City of Hampton, local, State, and Federal organizations involved in similar activities" (NASA, 2015, p. 8). When developing a plan for a crisis situation, for example, a NASA representative stated that:

> . . . basically you have to go with what you know. When you devise a plan, especially an active shooter, you implement it, you train your officers on how to do that, and then something changes so you have to reevaluate you have to say okay now . . . perfect example back in the day, you never went into an active shooter scenario with less than [pause] with less than two people. It was always as many as you can get. Then you will form up a pattern on how to go in diamond or whatever and then you go do that. Then officers . . . then after awhile people say wait a minute we don't have two officers in a vehicle anymore. Usually, it's just a one-patrol vehicle. It's the way it's been for many many years so how do we do that? So it evolved it continues to evolve, even today. I mean you [pause] before you could not go in unless you have a partner. Then officers would say wait a minute I'm standing out here waiting for my partner that might be two minutes out and I hear people getting killed. How the heck can I sit here and wait until I get . . . so then they started okay now we need to rethink. We need to go for solo officer entry and how do we teach our officers to do that? Totally different. (NASA, 2020)

When designing and implementing factors for the NASA police, there are geographical and jurisdictional considerations for which NASA (2015) LaRC has a formal agreement with the Hampton Police Department. Specifically, the

> . . . agreement is a living document that is reviewed and updated on a recurring ba-
> sis or when required to ensure the safety and security of both parties. The SSB also
> maintains an Interagency Agreement with Hampton Police Department SWAT for
> support requiring Specialized Police training and intervention. (p. 64)

In summary, NASA (2015) EMP plan, like the other educational institutions' operational safety plans, focuses on natural, technological, and manmade disasters. With NASA being a federal agency, Langley must follow the standards adopted by the federal government, which is the reason Langley utilizes NIMS as their source for EOP "existing best practices" (NASA, 2015, p. 7). Even though NASA is a federal entity, they are still obligated to coordinate with other local, state, and federal agencies due to jurisdictional boundaries in a manner not unlike a *quid pro quo* approach. Other unique aspects that set NASA's EOP apart from the other institutions in this study include very strict communication protocols that restrict information flow to organizations outside of NASA as well as a detailed three-tiered resource allocation framework. This is to say nothing of the brief threat assessment analysis of potential "meteor impacts" (NASA, 2015, p. 23).

Chapter Nine

Guiding Principles for Operational Safety Plans

The research questions in this study were examined through a multiple case study analysis in order to identify guiding principles, design factors, and candidate "best practices" associated with the design and implementation of operational safety plans at college-affiliated institutions. Data to answer the research questions were collected through document analysis of each institution's operational safety plan as well as follow-up interviews with emergency managers. Based on the research literature reviewed, a protocol list was created that included the following six themes (i.e., codes): Emergency Management, Resources, Coordination, Communication, Emergency Threat, and Training. These themes were organized as bins into which data were sorted in order to answer the following research questions.

Question #1: What principles guide the design of operational safety plans for college-affiliated institutions?

This question was explored through analysis of documents (i.e., operational safety plans) and interview materials from ISU, ODU, TCC, EVMS, and NASA. The document analysis protocol was based on a body of literature from which the researcher proposed six themes as to what principles guide the design of operational safety plans for the studied institutions. Using research and national emergency response frameworks (e.g., EMAP, NIMS, FEMA etc.), the following six themes were proposed as guiding principles for design of operational safety plans: *Emergency Management, Resources, Coordination, Communication, Emergency Threat, and Training.* After coding the operational safety plan documents, these six proposed themes were also used to analyze and code the interview material.

BUILD STRONG RELATIONSHIPS WITH EXPERTS (GUIDING PRINCIPLE #1)

The document analysis, along with the interview material, revealed a common thread supporting a guiding principle of emergency planners inviting a variety of experts to participate in the planning stage of their institution's operational safety plan. In fact, all the representatives from the studied institutions here noted that there should be strong relationships with experts in order to effectively design an operational safety plan. For example, an ISU representative stated,

> . . . make sure you develop a strong relationship with your local, state, and federal partners for emergency management. You'll be surprised at how they will tell you about grants opportunities, be willing to sponsor training programs on your campus. This brings people to your campus and it brings experts to your campus and that's the networking part of it. So you have to have a total of community engagement internally and externally. (ISU, 2020)

When asked to reflect on operational safety plan design recommendations they would make to others, an ODU representative shared:

> You have to have a team in place of people that are coming from the right areas and it can't even be necessarily the people you get along with its got to be everybody from all the different areas across campus that makes the place go I think that is and always be one of the major hallmarks in emergency management this the relationships and making sure to established and maintain in those relationships over the long term and if it's not with the person then it's with the people involved in making that function happen. If you don't have those . . . then it's impossible for the emergency manager to know everything about everything. We're a Jack-of-all-trades or Jill-of-all-trades, but a master of none and we're going to rely on subject matter expertise . . . (ODU, 2020)

One artifact of this guiding principle can be found in ISU's EOP plan, which states "The combined expertise and capabilities of ISU IMT and ISU First Responders, and city, county, and state First Responders will be required to *prepare for* [emphasis added], mitigate, respond to, and recover from emergencies" (ISU, 2019, p. 13).

KNOW YOUR ENVIRONMENTAL HAZARDS (GUIDING PRINCIPLE #2)

Emergency managers design their operational safety plans based on knowledge of their internal and external environments. This expertise consists of identifying 1) potential threats and hazards (i.e., natural, technological, and manmade) that can harm the college community and disrupt institutional operations, and then 2) resources available to mitigate and address effects of the crisis. Given that potential threats and available resources will likely change, emergency managers update these plans to reflect the fact that "the constantly changing hazard environment requires a commitment to process improvement" (ODU, 2019, p. 52). Furthermore, "An emergency or disaster may occur at any time of the day or night, weekend or holiday, with little or no warning, potentially causing significant loss of life, property damage, environmental and economic impact" (ODU, 2019, p. 21). All five institutions have outlined the threats and hazards that have the potential to disrupt their operations as shown in figure 9.1.

As part of the design of an operational safety plan, emergency managers develop annexes and appendices (i.e., detailed instructions of how to respond) for each potential threat/hazard identified in an institution's internal and external environments. To achieve this goal, ISU's emergency managers utilized an Emergency Response Gap Analysis:

> The objective of the Gap Analysis is to enhance the University's response readiness for the initial 72 hours of a disaster and their ability to support area first responders and outside agencies during an emergency. The analysis will be used to help establish the objectives for resource management. The analysis was performed based on the threats and hazards determined in the [Threat and Hazard Identification and Risk Assessment] THIRA (2013) and ISU's Multi-Campus Hazard Mitigation Plan (2014). However, ISU included other possible threats or hazards to ensure readiness for all hazards. (ISU, 2018a, p. 2)

Several institutions, including NASA (2015, p. 22) and EVMS (2017, p. 188), also utilized an assessment analysis. For example, ODU's (2019) CEMP states:

> . . . the University's existing Hazard Mitigation Plan (HMP) and a subsequent quantitative and qualitative threat, hazard identification, and risk assessment (THIRA) process involving whole of University community input, a series of potential threats and hazards to the institution have been identified. . . . Assessment parameters included historical occurrence/probability, impacts to human capital/facilities/the institution as a whole, and the existing preparedness posture. (p. 19)

In observing the process by which these five institutions identified their potential hazards and threats through document analysis, it became apparent there was variability in the degree to which each institution described their vulnerability analysis procedure. At one end of the continuum, ISU provided

Idaho State University	Old Dominion University	Tidewater Community College	Eastern Virginia Medical School	NASA Langley
Severe weather (winter and summer)	Active threat	Hurricane/ Tropical Storm	Floods (Storm Surge)	Toxic
Cyber/IT Disruption	Bomb threat/Explosion	Tornado/ Severe Weather	Floods (100-year)	Cryogenic Fuels and Oxidizers
Active Shooter	Civil Unrest/ Demonstration	Bomb threat	Hurricanes/ Tropical storms	Explosives
Wildfires/ Structural Fires	Code Adam	Fire	Winter storms	Pyrotechnics
Power Outages	Data Breach	Major Demonstration/ Civil Unrest	Tornados	High-Pressure Gas Systems
Civil disturbance or demonstration	Earthquake	Active Threat Response	Extreme Temperature	Vehicle Hardware
Hazardous Materials Incident	Extreme Temperature	Infrastructure Failure	Earthquakes	Radiological Materials
Utility failure/ Gas leak	Flooding, Hazardous Materials	Hazardous Materials Spill/Release	Crime	Oil Spills
Flood	Spill/Release	Shelter-in-Place	Hazmat release	Transportation Emergencies
Nuclear attack	Hurricane/Tropical Storm/Nor'easter	Evacuation	Radiological release	Aircraft Accidents
Earthquakes	Infrastructure Failure	Code Adam Alert	Biological release	Hurricanes
Structural Fires	Lightning	Cyber Security	Utility Failure (gas, power, sewer, telecom, water)	Tropical Depressions
Bombs/ Improvised Explosive Device (IED) Terrorism	Medical Emergency	Data Breach	Urban fire	Tornadoes and Severe Thunderstorms
Pandemic/ Epidemic	Public Health Incident		Public Health Emergencies	High Winds
Cyber/IT Disruption	Structure fire/ Arson			Flooding
	Threat of harm/ Criminal Activity			Snow and Ice Storms
	Severe Weather/ Tornado			Civil Disturbance
	Winter Storm			Bomb Threats
				Terrorist attack – Bombing
				Weapons of Mass Destruction incident
				Assault
				Robbery
				Shootings
				Kidnappings
				Hostage Barricade

Figure 9.1.   List of Potential Threats and Hazards in Selected Operational Safety

an entire separate document devoted to their Hazard and Threats (i.e., Resource and Emergency Response Gap Analysis), which provided extensive detail into the methods used and a copy of the survey sent to all stakeholders for their input. On the other end, TCC's operational safety plan did not include any references to how the institution arrived at its list of potential hazards and threats; it was unclear where else this information might be recorded. Descriptions of EVMS, ODU, and NASA's vulnerability analysis procedure plans fell somewhere between these two extremes.

OPERATIONAL SAFETY PLAN ENHANCEMENT
(GUIDING PRINCIPLE #3)

The operational safety plans are living documents in which "the constantly changing hazard environment requires a commitment to process improvement" (ODU, 2019, p. 52). Process improvement can refer to either enhancement of the operational safety plan for already identified hazards or expansion of the document to address new hazards not previously considered. Emergency managers review their plans after a specified time period as well as following annual exercises that train and recertify their first responders. ISU, ODU, EVMS, TCC, and NASA emergency plans are evaluated, updated, and tested annually. Evaluation data are generated from a debrief process whereby institutions managers determine what worked and what did not. In fact, ODU (2019) defines this process as a "Hot Wash: A discussion and/or evaluation of an agency's (or multiple agencies') performance following an exercise, training session, or incident/emergency/event" (p. A-12).

However, unexpected incidents that are not accounted for may arise and institutions will need to update their plans accordingly. While some representative institutions had annexes or appendices for public health contingencies, these primarily addressed known infectious agents (i.e., influenza, norovirus, tuberculosis, meningitis, etc.) (EVMS, 2017; ODU, 2019). However, none of the institutions were prepared for the novel coronavirus pandemic that they face now. There are eighteen known coronaviruses; however, the one in question is referred to COVID-19. In fact, it became clear through document analysis and interviews that these five institutions (and others) now have to update or include a new annex or appendix in their operational safety plans to deal with pandemics like the COVID-19 one. A TCC representative stated that:

> . . . updating those plans . . . to ensure that gets done every year as the executive staff present cabinet member changes or any new directives that come out say . . . from the state or VCCS and we did just do a new appendix to the CEMP for

pandemic response due to the Covid-19. We did not have anything in our plans for shutting the college down. We had to put that together pretty quick. (TCC, 2020)

One component of an institution's commitment to process improvement is flexibility, which was a term that frequently appeared in the studied operational safety plans. In ODU's (2019) CEMP plan, it stated, "The University's leadership recognizes that preventing, mitigating against, preparing for, responding to, and recovering from threats, incidents, and emergencies requires strategic policy guidance paired with operational flexibility to address the situation at hand" (p. 13). Flexibility allowed emergency managers to alter, adapt, and broaden the spectrum of unexpected incidents covered by their institution's operational safety plans. Since COVID-19 has radically altered worldwide norms, university officials strategically, methodically, and rapidly updated their emergency operations to account for an overnight/rapid shift of the entire institution from a primarily bricks-and-mortar existence to a primarily virtual one (i.e., synchronous and asynchronous formats). An ODU representative further stated:

> I understood that the way the plans need to be written allows for a lot of *flexibility* [emphasis added], scalability, and applicability regardless of size, scale, or scope of what's going on. That's all in keeping National Incident Management System doctrine we try to push that in all of the aspects we are writing so that we don't write ourselves into a corner. But really, COVID [-19] is a prime example for this. We did not have a formal extension plan of the Crisis Emergency Management Plan that specifically talked about pandemic outbreak response. . . . But there is a plan that already exists with student health services that relates to pandemic outbreak response. So essentially we kind of piggybacked off that one . . . (ODU, 2020)

The ISU representative also addressed COVID-19 in their interview, during which they shared, "Probably just COVID you know 19 just what I stated that we have developed a hybrid model on how we are going to address critical incidents that have a major impact on the whole campus you know we have totally changed that model" (ISU, 2020).

Another component addressed in the operational safety plans is scalability in terms of scaling a response to an incident such that the institution uses only the resources needed. In fact, all the operational safety plans developed annexes and appendices that specifically outline steps to take in the event of an emergency (e.g., hurricanes, data breach, active shooter, etc.). As the ODU representative stated above, emergency managers should account for ". . . flexibility, *scalability* [emphasis added], and applicability regardless of size, scale, or scope . . ." (ODU, 2020). In fact,

Depending on the type/scale/nature of the incident/emergency/event, not all members of the IMT [Incident Management Team] may be activated. For incident/emergency/event subject matter expertise, support, and/or resources, additional ad hoc members/liaisons may be appointed/ activated at the request of the Director of Emergency Management or designee. (ODU, 2019, p. 27)

At the same time, ISU's (2019) EOP stated, "All ISU IMT [Incident Management Team] members should be prepared to report to and operate from the EOC during a full-scale activation, even though all may not be needed" (p. 16). Lastly, EVMS' (2017) EOP stated, "The ERG [Emergency Response Group] can be scaled back or expanded as necessary depending on the needs of the disaster" (p. 10).

Lastly, applicability was also mentioned in the studied operational safety plans, ". . . flexibility, scalability, and *applicability* [emphasis added] regardless of size, scale, or scope . . ." (ODU, 2020), which meant that only specific resources would be matched with certain incidents. For example, EVMS' (2017) EOP read:

This plan is applicable to all EVMS departments and individuals that may be requested to provide assistance or conduct operations in the context of actual or potential emergencies or disasters at EVMS. It describes the fundamental policies, strategies, and general concept of operations to be used to control the emergency or disaster from its onset through the recovery phase. (pp. 1–2)

Meanwhile, ISU's (2019)

. . . EOP provides for a full emergency response by the University for any Incident. However, ISU will only activate sections of the EOC that are required to address the situation at that time. For example, a Level 1 disaster occurring on campus would require no activation of the EOC, but situations that are more serious would require increased activation. (p. 16)

Similarly, ODU (2019) CEMP stated, "The IMT [Incident Management Team] is augmented by supporting University departments, external agencies, and contractors, as applicable. All primary and supporting departments must be knowledgeable of overall CEMP operations" (p. 27). Finally, "NIMS [National Incident Management System] integrates existing best practices into a consistent, nationwide approach to domestic incident management that is applicable to all jurisdictional levels and across functional discipline in an all-hazards context" (NASA, 2015, p. 7).

For this particular research question, the objective was to identify guiding principles that aid in the design of operational safety plans for college-affiliated institutions. Based on document analysis of the operational safety plans and interviews with emergency management personnel, this study elucidated three guiding principles. Guiding principle #1, Build Strong Relationships with Experts, referred to development of rapport with local, state, and federal entities, which demonstrate features consistent with the Emergency Management and Coordination themes. Guiding principle #2, Know Your Environmental Hazards, described how emergency managers utilized gap analysis methods to decide what potential threats and hazards (i.e., natural, technological, and manmade) their operational safety plans would address. This principle most closely aligns with the Resources and Emergency Threat themes. Finally, guiding principle #3, Commitment to Operational Safety Plan Enhancement, referred to operational safety plan evaluation and improvement for both known and novel crises, which revealed attributes associated with the Communication and Coordination themes. Altogether, these three guiding principles for the design of operational safety plans provide insight into the factors necessary for their successful implementation.

Chapter Ten

Implementation Factors for Operational Safety Plans

Question #2: What factors found within college-affiliated education operational safety plans are critical for successful implementation?

This question too was investigated through analysis of documents (i.e., operational safety plans) and interview materials from the studied institutions: ISU, ODU, TCC, EVMS, and NASA. The document analysis also used themes from the developed protocol so as to determine what factors in operational safety plans are critical for successful implementation. To reiterate, the following six themes were proposed as essential for successful design and implementation of operational safety plans: Emergency Management, Resources, Coordination, Communication, Emergency Threat, and Training. These six themes were also used to analyze and code the interviews.

POLITICAL/LEGAL FACTORS (IMPLEMENTATION FACTOR #1)

In looking at the political and legal factors associated with implementation of operational safety plans, the institutions relied heavily on their general counsel for guidance and final review of these documents. In fact, all the operational safety plans had a promulgation statement signed by the institution's president, vice president, and chief of police. These statements reference the code of Virginia 23.1-804, which provides and mandates provisions for such plans. These documents must also comply with federal law. For example, an ISU representative stated, "Oh, yeah. Yeah there is always legal factors and all of our plans went through our review by the office of general counsel. We wanted to make sure that what we were saying we were doing was legal . . ." (ISU, 2020). In addition, the ODU representative shared,

... we vetted the plan through the office of general counsel and make sure they were happy with it. Humm, there is very little in the plan that is really coming at us from a . . . we can be sued thing. We are thinking about things like Clery compliance. That's going to be one of the biggest ones and that's the notification. A lot of that is going to fall at the Police department as well, but I think it's chapter 5 of the handbook . . . in the . . . of the Clery handbook that pertains to all things emergency notification. We try to have enough guidance in there that is going to provide for that . . . (ODU, 2020)

Furthermore, a representative from NASA shared, "I'm sure you know they have to abide by some regulations OSHA [Occupational Safety and Health Administration] or whoever or whatever and then make sure that it's vetted . . ."

Political factors were also salient for some institutions while not for others when implementing operational safety plans. To illustrate, a TCC representative shared the following political factor reference campus safety at his college:

... we have contract security and they are hands off. They . . . have no stopping or arrest powers so we have to write our response to certain crises knowing that all we can do is sit back and wait for the police to arrive. Which has led to the reality that we need to commission a police force and have our own independent TCC police force, and we are heavily involved in that right now . . . the new president commissioned a committee to study this and meet with stakeholders around the college and discuss it and kind of interview students and faculty and get their feedback and what it would be like to have an armed police force on campus, but we're definitely moving that way. (TCC, 2020)

During a follow-up conversation with the same TCC representative, he provided an update on the police force proposal: "Placed on indefinite hold due to the national issues surrounding police" (TCC, personal communication, 2020).

On the other hand, however, an ISU representative posited that,

... from a political standpoint, politics didn't really have any play in anything that we did. We didn't have any situations where there was a VP or the president wanted this way or that way. They actually trusted us to come up with the best protocols, procedures, and guidance on how to mitigate, plan, prepare, respond, and recover from critical incidents . . . (ISU, 2020)

The representative of EVMS concurred, sharing that ". . . we had to have established one [pause] we knew we're not violent and so getting the MOUs [Memoranda of Understanding] and agreements and jurisdiction with the City of Norfolk and those resources politically we really didn't have a whole lot of problems . . ." (EVMS, 2020).

FINANCIAL FACTORS (IMPLEMENTATION FACTOR # 2)

Financial factors were considered more often in the implementation of operational safety plans. In fact, all of these institutional documents contained artifacts resulting from the effects of these financial factors, including annexes and appendices that provide directions regarding resources, equipment, etc. ODU's (2019) ESF (Emergency Support Function) annexes specifically address resource allocation, management, and recovery. For example, ODU's (2019) ESF 5 states that the emergency managers will "assist in the provision of training on disaster-related financial management procedures for University departments . . . [and] provide staffing for the Finance/Administration Section of the EOC [Emergency Operations Center]" (p. A-5-6). In addition, ESF 7 stipulates that, ". . . [it] will maintain a list of anticipated essential material resources and a list of potential suppliers in order to obtain resources more expeditiously during a major disaster or emergency" (p. A-7-2). Finally, ODU's (2019) ESF 11 states that, "agencies will document costs of operations and submit to the EOC Finance/Administration Section for the purposes of reimbursement" (p. A-11-4). Document analysis indicated that all institutions had annexes, appendices, or both that dealt with financial factors, which are listed in figure 10.1.

In interviewing the ISU representative about any financial constraints on their operational safety plan, he stated, "There were no financial challenges. We did not have to sacrifice anything to get something we felt was important. Our institution provided the funding that was necessary" (ISU, 2020). Meanwhile, when the ODU representative was asked about funding for their operational safety plan, he stated:

List of Operational Safety Plan Annexes and Appendices for Financial Factors				
Idaho State University (ISU)	Old Dominion University (ODU)	Tidewater Community College (TCC)	Eastern Virginia Medical School (EVMS)	NASA Langley
ANX-Admin and Financial	ESF 5. Emergency Management	Section IV Campus Command Business Manager	ESF 5. Emergency Management	Management System (NIMS)-Logistics and Administration
ANX-Damage Assessment Annex	ESF 7. Resource Management	Section IV Campus Command Notiication and Assessment	ESF 7. Logistics Management and Resource Support	Tasks-Emergency Manager (EM)
ANX-Local Mutual Aid_Multi-Agency Coordination	ESF 11. Resource Protection	Section IV Campus Command Recover Actions	ESF 17. Volunteers and Donations	Tasks-Office of Strategic Analysis, Communications and Business Development (OSACB), News Media Teams (NMT), Public Affairs, (PA)
ANX-Volunteer and Donation Management		Section V District Command Emergency Operations Center Vice President for Finance	Appendix 5. Financial Recovery	

Figure 10.1. **List of Operational Safety Plan Annexes and Appendices for Financial Factors**

. . . it needs a massive overhaul, and that is something that absent either additional staff or grant funding, which I've been trying to apply for with each and every federally declared disaster or just asking for operational funding and to get that . . . that's you know several 10s of 1000s of dollars to get a contractor to come in and support us with that effort. There's a lot I mean we're trying to check the boxes. We actually have a matrix that we keep and we are slowly poking away at it and getting ready for accreditation. And also there is a financial component to that too. It ain't cheap to become accredited because you have to pay for an all-inclusive visit by a team to come here so it's between $5,000 to $10,000 dollars, which normally isn't bad, but right now given what we're dealing with [referring to COVID-19] and anticipating 15 percent budget cuts across the board it's going to be harder to swallow . . . (ODU, 2020)

The ODU representative continued by observing that ". . . we wanted to make sure that all things financial were accounted for . . . we follow what the state does and feds do and even the City of Norfolk in designing the plan to make sure that it kinda fit the model that is prescribed by the National Incident Management System" (ODU, 2020). The TCC representative discussed their financial factors through the lens of a current safety issue facing the college; that is, conversion of campus security to a police department:

Oh yeah, [laughs] everything is driven by money, and the money really is the speed bump for the police transition because you have to figure out how to balance maintaining that contract security presence and then hiring and developing a police force so that is . . . one of the things we're working with, but the benefit is that when we transition fully over to the police force and we're done with contract we'll save about $500,000 dollars a year . . . out of 4 million, that's an eighth; it's a big savings. (TCC, 2020)

The EVMS representative provided a detailed response when it came to his institution's financial factors and operational safety plan:

You know we like to say hey when it comes to safety and everything money should not be an object, but at the end of the day it is. One equipment for my group . . . I don't got a SWAT team, but we have equipment in case we have to respond to a situation, ballistic shields, vests, we have a 40 caliber that matches our hand guns it's a 40 caliber carbine that handles a Glock magazine so it's all coordinated. We have that equipment; we do . . . some training . . . there are those types of events as far as financially secondly uh there're always expenses involved coordination for hurricanes . . . the active shooting stuff, but hurricanes making sure they understood the pay . . . all of my employees because we go to 12 hour rotations and everyone is basically on campus . . . during a hurricane in . . . 24-hour[s] before it's due to hit until it clears up and they work rotating shifts and [I] want them to understand how the pay works out, how the compensation, keeping track of that and that it would be incurred overtime on that and those types of financial resources had to be taken into consideration . . . making sure that everyone understood there are added expenses during emergencies and what have you and during recovery so it came into play, but it was never a totally restricting factor for having an effective plan because it's more costly not to have an effective plan than the cost . . . to have it work . . . (EVMS, 2020)

Finally, the NASA representative indicated that,

> When it comes to safety, the sky's the limits, you know, within reason sometimes. You know like I said they have a plan, they want to do something. It's all about safety and if it's going to cost something then they weigh that as well. However, safety is, in anything, is paramount . . . I'm sure they have quality folks that say, "okay tamp 'er down you might not need to get to that level right now," you know, even though you're asking, you know, for the sky. You might have to bring it down to the mountain range. (NASA, 2020)

OPERATIONAL FACTORS (IMPLEMENTATION FACTOR #3)

Document and interview analysis also revealed several Operational factors that were important to the implementation of operational safety plans. Two identified factors in this analysis were "do the institutions have an Emergency Operations Center (EOC)?" and "who are designated to be on the incident management team?" All five institutional operational safety plans had dedicated space describing where a primary (and sometimes a secondary) EOC would be located as well as the designated personnel assigned to the incident management team. For example, according to the ISU's (2019) Emergency Operational Plan,

> Incident command and Emergency Operations Center (EOC) positions must be fluid in order to meet the complexity of an Incident. When an Incident arises, the University President or his/her designee will activate the EOP through the disaster declaration process or EOC activation. The Incident Commander (IC), in coordination with the EOC Manager, will implement the EOP in accordance with the level of emergency based on priorities that include life safety, preservation of property and environment, restoration of essential utilities and functions, and a return to normal operations. . . . The size, staffing, and equipping of the EOC will depend on the magnitude and complexity of the Incident. The IC will determine which positions are needed and notify the EOC Manager and appropriate ISU personnel, as needed. All ISU IMT members should be prepared to report to and operate from the EOC during a full-scale activation, even though all may not be needed. ISU IMT members should bring their own radios and/

or cellular phones, and other items necessary to carry out assignments. . . . In accordance with standard emergency management system planning, ISU has established several ISU EOC locations. (pp. 13–16)

During the interview with the ISU representative, he further elaborated,

> I think that the biggest operational factor was when we first got started we did not have an EOC in our building so we had to designate a primary EOC and then an alternate EOC on our campus. The incident management team was way too large when I first got here. I think we had 40 some people on the incident management [laughs] team, and these people . . . that's why we had large venues for EOC and so I actually cut that down to 15 people because the people on the incident management team were actually the people that would be out in the field dealing with the critical incident so from an operational standpoint, we cut back on the incident management team and we have to find an EOC. (ISU, 2020)

Meanwhile, for ODU, the driving operational factor involves the goal of protecting continuity of operations for all campus stakeholders during an emergency. To achieve this objective, the emergency management team uses the guidelines from the National Incident Management System (NIMS) when implementing their plan. According to an ODU representative,

> . . . we wanted to make sure that all things . . . were accounted for in the plan so actually . . . make sure that it kinda fit the model that is prescribed by the National Incident Management System. What we used is the Emergency Support Functional Model so we break up campus into 15, 17, and 19 different ESFs where we say academics fits in this bucket; research fits in this bucket; the resource management . . . fits into this bucket and so on and so forth for public safety and security and emergency management and facility management . . . and infrastructure all those kinds of things generally align with the nationally recommended ESF model so . . . we wanted to account for all of the key functional areas that make the university that go on a regular basis. . . . They also have a respected area called a primary business function that plugs into the university's overall mission when we are talking about the university's continuity plan. . . . We also look at things from the continuing operations or be able to reconstitute operations through our continuity plan. . . . We did look at things for the operation of the university. We wanted to make sure that the plan reflected what we're doing here and it's not just something off the shelf that we're grabbing from somebody else . . . the representatives and our go-to-people on campus for each of these functional areas are the key drivers that make sure that plan as written whether it's the general plan or it's specific to their functional area are absolutely critical and making sure that we have something customized to our operations and I should also add that when we wrote the plan we wanted to make sure that it was regional . . . (ODU, 2020)

Similar to ODU, EVMS's representative also acknowledged that different campus locations had unique operational needs, requiring unique allocation of resources during an emergency to address this particular factor in maintaining continuity of operations. He explicated that,

> Operational again yeah you had to consider that because one even though technically the EVMS is a nonprofit organization and there are revenue sources . . . our clinical operations have disrupted things would be moving of people . . . we do have an apartment complex, which is geared for students, but it's not it's more for an apartment complex management thing as opposed to a dormitory, but we still had to find place/locations for students. We had two locations if this office goes down, if payroll goes . . . where is payroll going to be handled if Smith Rogers, which is one building that is subject to flooding. If that shuts down, how where they transferring this from where's that transfer so those types of considerations were given in agreement . . . put in place ahead of time on how to mitigate those type of things to keep things running as best as it can and now if a clinical area say Hofheimer Hall became damaged to where they could not provide medical services they had alternative offices in Sentara they had some out at Princess Anne at Glenn Mitchell. They had different offices they could reroute patients to and what have you and services so we did have to look at those operational things, what is the impact, how are we going to be able to work that out. I know its getting into the continuity of operations plan, but it also operational understanding those things as far as getting that type of thing going, and what facilities might need additional protection or what have you, just like no need of sandbagging things over at Williams Hall because it never has flooded over, but Smith Rodgers over there floods all the time so where do we put those resources ahead of time knowing that and getting those distributed and making sure that there especially for things you have time to prepare for that was for once again weather events is our biggest, have been our biggest headaches as far as emergency operations. (EVMS, 2020)

TCC, like the other institutions studied here, must consider the operational factor of having multiple campuses when implementing its operational safety plan. In fact, technology (i.e., cameras, radios, etc.) is critical when attempting to safeguard a large geographical area of campus real estate. To illustrate, a TCC representative stated:

> You know, having four campuses and locations all around Hampton Roads is a huge impact on how we operate. The director, you know, and future chief of police, it's not like he's right on campus. And so coordinating any kind of response that's not at the district office gets difficult 'cause the EOC get stood up here at district and we're really relying on technology and communications equipment to kind of control the scene and we're not . . . never going to be right there. And I think right there . . . it's one of the challenges that we have. We do not have a

camera system we are in the process of having a feasibility study done right now
for a college wide security system.

Lastly, the NASA representative shared the following:

> Operational factors? . . . Well, you have to consider that all the time operational
> wise because even though you might have an operation A to Z, D and E might
> have to shift. You know, so there are contingency that you have to have built in
> the event . . . now you can't predict everything that can go FUBAR; however,
> you try to mitigate that best practice, experience, those things will dictate, you
> know, how to go forward with that.

OTHER FACTORS TO CONSIDER
(IMPLEMENTATION FACTOR #4)

Other factors to consider were the organizational culture in which institutions implement their operational safety plans and the environment in which
the institution exists. Individuals from ISU and TCC both mentioned aspects
of their unique cultures as salient factors for implementation. On one hand,
ISU's (2020) representative shared that,

> . . . Our campus has always been very supportive of emergency management.
> . . . You call and they just come out. . . . From the president, the VPs, everyone
> . . . you call them and say we need or whatever, they are there for the campus
> community. When we have meetings for the incident management team, the
> building managers, the floor marshals, they show up for meetings and I'm not
> used to so I found that we had a lot support here that I was not used to having.

On the other hand, TCC's (2020) representative stated,

> Culture. [pause] Definitely culture of the college and there you know there's
> just some people that see us as really embellishing the term community college
> and inviting everybody to come on campus, walk in our buildings, we're open,
> come see us, and these days that doesn't fly. You know, we've seen ever since
> the Virginia Tech shootings and all these other shootings, it's no longer feasible
> . . . that's our biggest challenge college wide is the culture.

In parallel, the ODU (2020) representative discussed a unique environmental
factor that they consider when implementing their operational safety plan.
He expounded,

> . . . We are a city within a city. We have a residential student population;
> we have research 50 million dollar plus research expenditures; we have on
> campus dining; we have an open campus in a state where it's okay to openly

carry weapons. We have minors that are on campus; we have daycares on campus; we have of course all of the natural hazard phenomena that we have to deal with. We have the world's largest naval base up the street. We have truck traffic on Hampton Blvd. We have a large coal terminal just to our west we are . . . anything that pops off that is kinda of the incident du jour whether it's an active threat; whether it's COVID [-19]; whether whatever it may be those things garner our attention. . . . What partnerships and interdependencies with vendors, with utility companies, with all those kind of things . . . with food service and fuel providers. We recognize we can't do everything ourselves when we have snow events. That's why we bought plows for a couple of vehicles because sometimes if it's not on Hampton Blvd then it's not going to get plowed. In colder winters that can set us back a considerable amount of time. So it's kind of . . . the resources that we have and what we should do on campus, what we can pull from our partners in the city or from anybody else or what we need to get from higher levels.

The objective of this research question was to identify implementation factors that aided in the execution of operational safety plans at college-affiliated institutions. Analysis of the operational safety plan documents and interviews with emergency management personnel revealed four categories of implementation factors. Implementation Factor #1, Political/Legal Factors, showed that all institutional operational safety plans are vetted through a legal entity (e.g., an Office of General Counsel) for guidance and final review in order to reduce or mitigate liability. Some institutions mentioned that they did not have any political issues, while some did experience external political influences affecting internal emergency management issues (e.g., conversion of a security company to a police force). These components align with the Emergency Management, Coordination, and Resources protocol themes. Implementation Factor #2, Financial Factors, included issues related to resource allocation, management, and recovery, which were addressed in annexes and appendices found in these institutional operational safety plans. These factors aligned with Resources and Emergency Management themes. Implementation Factor #3, Operational Factors, included establishment of operational safety logistics (e.g., members to be named to the Incident Management Team) as well as guidelines for protecting unique institutional assets during a crisis. The factors in this category were most closely associated with the Emergency Management, Emergency Threat, Coordination, and Communication themes. Finally, Implementation Factor #4, Other Factors to Consider, comprised the unique institutional cultures and environments in which operational safety plans are implemented, which best matched with the Emergency Management theme. Taken together, the three previously identified guiding principles and these four implementation factors made it possible to identify candidate "best practices" for operational safety plans.

Chapter Eleven

Best Practices for Operational Safety Plans

Question #3: What are the "best practices" for operational safety plans that are utilized by college-affiliated institutions?

This research question was explored through analysis of documents (i.e., operational safety plans) and interview transcripts. In addition, a document analysis protocol was used, which had previously proposed six themes for determining "best practices" utilized by ISU, ODU, TCC, EVMS, and NASA based on published literature. To reiterate, this protocol used research studies and national emergency response frameworks (e.g., EMAP, NIMS, etc.), which yielded themes of Emergency Management, Resources, Coordination, Communication, Emergency Threat, and Training as guidelines to determine candidate "best practices" for operational safety plans. After coding the operational safety plan documents, these six proposed themes were also used to analyze and code the interview material.

TRAINING (BEST PRACTICE #1)

The institutions studied included framework objectives for preventing, mitigating, preparing, responding, and recovering from emergencies. In order to achieve these objectives of preventing, mitigating, and preparing, institutions enact annual training for their first responders, administrators, etc. For example, ISU's (2019) Emergency Operations Plan states that,

ISU's Department of Public Safety will coordinate and provide appropriate levels of training to administration, faculty, and staff to ensure that individuals, based on their campus roles and responsibilities, are adequately trained in emergency management and incident response concepts and principles, thereby maintaining compliance with core national emergency response standards found in NIMS. (p. 38)

ISU (2019) further stipulates the following components of their training and exercise program:

- Meet NIMS compliance requirements;
- Provide NIMS core curriculum to ensure a NIMS/ICS baseline is established, which provides a foundation for higher-level training as required;
- Conduct training and exercise needs assessment. An Exercise/Training Needs Assessment form will be distributed to the Emergency Management Committee and IMT for completion every four (4) years. Using the results from the assessment tool, the Emergency Manager and the Training and Exercise Committee will identify any training requirements or requests;
- Include training and exercises provided through county and regional LEPCs;
- Utilize the building block approach. In accordance with goals and objectives, the EM conducts discussion-based or operational exercises across the institution to: 1) demonstrate new capabilities gained through training; 2) validate plans, policies, and procedures; 3) demonstrate proficiency on equipment; and 4) address improvement planning through application of lessons learned. Some type of exercise will be held at least annually, with full scale exercises held at least once every two (2) to three (3) years;
- Ensure all exercises are Department of Homeland Security Exercise and Evaluation Program (HSEEP) compliant;
- Complete an AAR with an IP for each exercise using the HSEEP AAR/IP template. The AAR/IP will be completed by ISU employees involved in the exercise along with any local partners/agencies involved in the exercise. Any training or other deficiencies found through the AAR/IP will be forwarded to the Emergency Manager to address and schedule the needed training or improvements;
- Address all-Hazards and Threats through objective-based exercises using directives found in FEMA's Target Capabilities List. (pp. 38–39)

Finally, ISU's (2019) Incident Management Team (IMT) and First responders will be provided training on current responsibilities by completing the following courses:

- IS 100 Introduction to ICS
- IS 700 NIMS, an Introduction
- IS 200 ICS for Single Resources and Initial Action Incidents. (p. 39)

In the interview with ISU's (2020) representative, he shared as it relates to training,

I would say keeping your incident management team trained. . . . So whether you have the fire department comes out and shows them how to use a fire extinguisher, CPR training, you have a person come in and talk about environmental health and safety . . . keeping them you know active with exercises, and running policies, and . . . you will lose them if you don't train them . . . they need to have the basic ICS training and then there needs to be training for our campus . . . be willing to sponsor training programs on your campus.

In review of ODU's (2019) CEMP, it outlines a training and exercise plan, which reads:

The training program consists of an annual needs assessment in the form of a Training and Exercise Planning Workshop (TEPW–conducted during the September Emergency Management Advisory Committee meeting), curriculum (detailed in the Multi-Year Training and Exercise Plan [MYTEP]), course evaluations, and records of training. Training is regularly scheduled and conducted with the overall goals and objectives of the training program, and is based on the training needs assessment/TEPW, and internal and external requirements and mandates, and addresses deficiencies identified in the corrective action process. (p. 50)

The exercise, evaluation, and corrective action program regularly tests the knowledge,

skills and abilities, and experience of personnel expected to serve in an emergency response/coordination capacity as well as the plans, policies, procedures, equipment, and facilities that constitute the University's emergency management program. Periodic reviews, testing, post-incident reports, lessons learned, performance evaluations, exercises, and real-world events serve to evaluate plans, procedures, and capabilities of the University's emergency management program. The products of these evaluations are documented and disseminated with appropriate program stakeholders and selected partners. (p. 51)

The operational safety plans for EVMS, TCC, and NASA also contained language indicating that training and exercises would be conducted at least annually.

INSTITUTION'S OPERATIONAL SAFETY PLAN REVIEW (BEST PRACTICE # 2)

EVMS (2017), ISU (2019), NASA (2015), ODU (2019), and TCC (2017) emergency managers implement a review process for maintaining their operational safety plans as current. Institutions' (i.e., ISU, ODU, EVMS, and NASA) emergency managers conduct their operational safety plan review annually. For example, ISU's (2019) operational safety plan states:

All emergency plans will be evaluated and updated on an annual basis. These plans include:

- Emergency Operations Plan (EOP) and any supplemental plans or annexes;
- Continuity of Operations (COOP);
- Continuity of Government (COG);
- Multi-Campus Hazard Mitigation Plan (exception every 2 years);
- Multi-Year Training and Exercise Plan;
- EM Multi-Year Strategic Plan;
- Building Emergency Action Plans.

The Emergency Manager will be the lead on all plan reviews and updates. This person will have knowledge of all current policies and procedures of the Emergency Management Program (p. 41).

In addition, ODU's (2019) plan showed that, "In accordance with *Code of Virginia* §23.1-804, this CEMP will be updated annually. A comprehensive review and revision will be completed every four years with certification in writing to the Virginia Department of Emergency Management (VDEM)" (pp. 49–50). EVMS' (2017) operational safety plan also outlined that,

> The EVMS Emergency Manager is responsible for the development and maintenance of the EVMS EOP. The Emergency Manager will, on an annual basis, solicit and incorporate suggestions and changes from the EVMS Executive Leadership and Department Directors, as needed. The Emergency Manager must submit all changes for final approval by the Vice President for Administration and Finance prior to adoption. (p. 22)

Moreover, NASA's (2015) operational safety plan read: "This plan is unclassified and will be reviewed at least annually" (p. 11). Conversely, TCC's (2017) operational safety plan read: "In accordance with Code of Virginia §23-9.2:9, this CEMP will be updated regularly as needed. A comprehensive review and revision will be conducted every four years with certification in writing to the Virginia Department of Emergency Management (VDEM)" (p. 46). Interestingly, the NASA (2020) representative shared when asked about the utilization of NIMS for benchmarking stated,

> Humm, I don't know. I think maybe if it's not broken, don't fix it. If they have procedures in place, paperwork, and ways of doing things it's always good to reevaluate, but going in and trying to change everything that's proven that works then why would you? You know so . . . there are times when it has to be updated and there is a new system that comes out or a new way of doing things . . . I'm running into that because I'm a 100 years old and this technical stuff

is killing me you know so I have to learn how to adapt to that and sometime for me it's frustrating.

Finally, the five institutions complete an After Action Review/Report (AAR) after a major event (i.e., natural, manmade, or technological) or a training exercise. ISU (2019) indicated that they will complete an AAR after a crisis as well as,

> Complete an AAR with an IP [Improvement Plan] for each exercise using the HSEEP [Department of Homeland Security Exercise and Evaluation Program]
>
> AAR/IP template. The AAR/IP will be completed by ISU employees involved in the exercise along with any local partners/agencies involved in the exercise. Any training or other deficiencies found through the AAR/IP will be forwarded to the Emergency Manager to address and schedule the needed training or improvements. (p. 39)
>
> ODU (2019), EVMS (2017), TCC (2017), and NASA (2015), however, only appear to complete an After Action Review/Report (AAR) after a crisis.

EXTERNAL RESOURCES (BEST PRACTICE #3)

All five institutions in this study utilized external resources to guide in the design and implementation of their operational safety plans. To begin with, the institutions incorporated standards from National Incident Management System (NIMS), the Incident Command System (ICS), Emergency Management Accreditation Program (EMAP), Occupational Safety and Health Administration (OSHA), Virginia Department of Emergency Management (VDEM), Federal Emergency Management Agency (FEMA), State Council of Higher Education for Virginia (SCHEV), and the Department of Homeland Security (DHS). ISU's Emergency Operational Plan states "This EOP utilizes the Incident Command System (ICS), and is in compliance with the National Incident Management System (NIMS)." Furthermore, in an interview with an ISU (2020) representative, he shared that,

> . . . Idaho State in 2015 . . . had just become accredited by EMAP and we were the second institution of higher ED to get that designation behind Virginia Tech . . . I served as a mediator for FEMA's higher ed symposium that's an annual event I served on several national committees dealing with emergency management . . . we just looked at . . . the overall guidance that FEMA gives. . . . REMS TA Centers [Readiness and Emergency Management for Schools Technical Assistance Center] . . . on how to develop high quality emergency operations plan, so we use that guidance from 2013 so everything we use kind of came up from

FEMA and NIMS and from any documents that focus on higher ed; those were the benchmarks that we used.

The ISU representative advised that emergency personnel should "make sure you develop a strong relationship with your local, state, and federal partners for emergency management" (ISU, 2020).

ODU's (2019) CEMP:

> . . . employs elements of the National Incident Management System (NIMS) and the Incident Command System (ICS), both of which serve to provide a nationwide template to enable Federal/State/local/tribal governments and external partners to work together effectively and efficiently to prevent, mitigate against, prepare for, respond to, and recover from domestic incidents regardless of cause, size, or complexity. The use of NIMS and ICS at ODU facilitates the University's ability to communicate internally among ODU departments, Higher Education Centers, and other locations, coordinate response actions with local jurisdictions and external emergency response agencies, and integrate into an expanding incident management system for local, regional, State, or Federal emergencies. (p. 13)

An ODU's (2020) representative shared that

> . . . we have to . . . comply with the regulations, code of Virginia 23.1-804 the buck stops . . . starts and stops with that one from a governing standpoint. NIMS certainly informs it. . . . There is lots of other guidance that exists that FEMA has developed. There is one called A Guide for Developing High Quality Emergency Operation plans for Institutions of Higher Education that's a FEMA document. There's, of course, an EMAP guidance Emergency Management Accreditation Program that we are working to get our program to that point. It's just going to take us a while, but we are trying to build using that as an industry standard and practice . . . stuff that applies from OSHA . . . CALEA, commission on accreditation for law enforcement agencies. If other people can get a beam for having their stuff plugged in and then that helps them with their accreditation then we want to focus on that.

In review of EVMS' EOP (2017) it states, "This plan is modeled after the National Response Framework (NRF) and incorporates the National Incident Management System (NIMS) to facilitate coordination between responding departments and agencies" (p. 2). The EVMS' (2020) representative shared,

> Basically initially we had hired an outside consultant firm to develop our emergency operational plan. . . . And, and we worked with them and that was fine, but then kind of [pause] we had to readapt and readjust that plan because they did include ICS in a fashion, but they tried to tailor it so specifically to EVMS

that it didn't follow the same general principles so we just kind of got away from that and then VDEM put out a thing where they had a specific model they wanted the institutions of higher education to follow and we just felt it was our best interest to follow that protocol and that's what we did so we really didn't banter around a whole lot of other ones initially with myself, our emergency manager coming from the Norfolk Fire Department, and the Norfolk Police Department and a lot of my staff coming from the various local police departments have all been trained in NIMS and ICS and what have you so we just felt like that was the best way to go. . . . Once that other one was getting a little more convoluted we kind of decided nah we need follow that then the Virginia Department of Emergency Management came and said "here's a template that we really like for all our institutions to kind of follow this template" and this fit right in on what we were saying with the NIMS and what have you.

TCC's (2017) CEMP "complies with the Code of Virginia Title 23 and Title 44 and with Commonwealth of Virginia Executive Orders 41(2011) and complies with the National Incident Management System as implemented in the National Response Framework" (p. v). Additionally, the TCC (2020) representative was asked if he and his team utilized any protocols from NIMS, EMAP, etc. for benchmarking in which he stated,

[Long pause] definitely not something I'm educated on with those terms and stuff like that. The CEMP that we have is an inherited document driven by VDEM guidelines and the VCCS guidelines. I believe there is some SCHEV oversight on it as well because we're an institution of higher learning. So we submit it every year to the system office and get it approved every year so obviously we're maintaining that document in compliance with the state guidelines and federal guidelines.

Lastly, NASA Langley (2015) EMP reads,

NIMS will be employed as the structure for command, control, coordination, and recovery for all hazards incidents at LaRC. It will also support the Emergency Support Functions listed under the National Response Plan and LaRC LPRs and Appendices. The Department of Homeland Security is the Office of Preparedness and Response (OPR) that establishes a national policy for Federal Departments and Agencies to identify and prioritize critical infrastructure and to protect them from terrorist attacks. NIMS will be the standard on-scene, all-hazards incident management system for firefighters, hazardous materials teams, rescuers, security, and emergency medical teams. NIMS integrates existing best practices into a consistent, nationwide approach to domestic incident management that is applicable to all jurisdictional levels and across functional disciplines in an all-hazards context.

The NASA (2020) representative shared that the EMP design is above his pay grade and that, "I'm sure you know they have to abide by some regulations OSHA or whoever or whatever and then make sure that it's vetted . . ."

These institutions, furthermore, have developed external partnerships with federal, state, and city agencies for the purpose of securing needed resources during a crisis. It stated in ISU's (2019) EOP that " the overall objective is to ensure the effective management of emergency efforts involved . . . coordinating and maintaining liaisons with appropriate federal, state, and other local governmental agencies and appropriate private sector organizations" (p. 10). In addition, "Response to a major Incident will progress from local, to regional, to state, to federal involvement" (ISU, 2019, p. 13). In ODU's (2019) CEMP, it stated,

> To address these hazards, the University has developed the ODU Crisis and Emergency Management Plan (CEMP) using best practice guidance from Federal, State, and local sources and the higher education sector to organize prevention, mitigation, preparedness, response, and recovery activities for incidents, emergencies, and events at ODU. (p. 13)

EVMS' EOP (2017) reads: "Assistance from city, county, state, and federal agencies and from volunteer and private organizations may be available to supplement School resources . . . EVMS may also be available to assist city, county, and federal agencies as requested" (p. 4). Furthermore, EVMS' EOP (2017) stated:

> When the response to a disaster or emergency exceeds School resources, assistance may be requested from the City of Norfolk, other public and private institutions and vendors, and state and federal agencies. County, state, and federal assistance must be requested through the City of Norfolk Office of Emergency Management. (p. 6)

The EVMS' (2020) representative stated, for example, that,

> . . . if we need to call help in from Norfolk Police sometimes or the Fire, or other universities or what have you having that same protocol; the two hospitals use the same systems we have to interface it just makes sense in a way that it can be expanded and contracted it to meet the various types of hazards we may face.

TCC's (2017) CEMP . . . is modeled after the National Response Framework (NRF) and incorporates the National Incident Management Systems (NIMS) to facilitate coordination between responding departments and agencies. TCC cooperates with local, state, and federal emergency management agencies and other responders in the development, implementation, and execution of emergency response plans (p. 2).

Finally, NASA Langley's EMP (2015) stated that the

> Implementation of the procedures set forth in the EMP will be considered when the emergency is likely to be beyond the response and recovery capability of responding forces or has the potential to become a large-scale disaster involving numerous Federal, State, and local Agencies and forces . . . Mutual Aid Agreements allow one jurisdiction to provide resources, facilities, services, and other required support to another jurisdiction during an incident . . . NIMS compliance activities require jurisdictions to participate in and promote intrastate and interagency mutual aid agreements with private sector and non-governmental organizations. The Incident Command System (ICS) is used to organize both near-term and long-term field-level operations for a broad spectrum of emergencies, from small to complex incidents, both natural and manmade. ICS is used by all levels of government, Federal, State, local, and tribal. (pp. 7–8)

RESPONSE FRAMEWORK (BEST PRACTICE #4)

These institutions utilized annexes, appendices, or both that clearly outlined instructions on how to prepare for, respond to, or recover from a particular type of incident (e.g., natural, manmade, or technological). Using ISU as a representative example, each annex or appendix defined a particular incident Title (e.g., hurricane, active shooter, etc.), Purpose Statement, Scope, Concepts of Operations, Roles and Responsibilities, Notification Procedure, Response Procedure, Forms and Procedures for Record Keeping During Disasters, and Documentation Procedures (ISU, 2019). Figure 11.1 lists the annexes and appendices for all potential incidents identified by each institution in this study.

LEVERAGE INTELLECTUAL ASSETS (BEST PRACTICE #5)

Concurrently, the operational safety plans for all five institutions clearly delineated an Emergency Operation Center (EOC) and instructions for activating, staffing, and operating in response to a crisis (i.e., before, during, and after). This results from soliciting input from campus and outside sources of expertise during the design and review of operational safety plans. Furthermore, each college-affiliated institution prescribes which subject matter experts will comprise the Incident Management Team (IMT) that will oversee emergency

ISU Total: 15	ODU Total: 18	TCC Total: 13	EVMS Total: 14	NASA Total: 25
Severe weather (winter and summer)	Active threat	Hurricane/ Tropical Storm	Floods (Storm Surge)	Toxic
Cyber/IT Disruption	Bomb threat/Explosion	Tornado/ Severe Weather	Floods (100-year)	Cryogenic Fuels and Oxidizers
Active Shooter	Civil Unrest/ Demonstration	Bomb threat	Hurricanes/ Tropical storms	Explosives
Wildfires/ Structural Fires	Code Adam	Fire	Winter storms	Pyrotechnics
Power Outages	Data Breach	Major Demonstration/ Civil Unrest	Tornados	High-Pressure Gas Systems
Civil disturbance or demonstration	Earthquake	Active Threat Response	Extreme Temperature	Vehicle Hardware
Hazardous Materials Incident	Extreme Temperature	Infrastructure Failure	Earthquakes	Radiological Materials
Utility failure/ Gas leak	Flooding, Hazardous Materials	Hazardous Materials Spill/Release	Crime	Oil Spills
Flood	Spill/Release	Shelter-in-Place	Hazmat release	Transportation Emergencies
Nuclear attack	Hurricane/Tropical Storm/Nor'easter	Evacuation	Radiological release	Aircraft Accidents
Earthquakes	Infrastructure Failure	Code Adam Alert	Biological release	Hurricanes
Structural Fires	Lightning	Cyber Security	Utility Failure (gas, power, sewer, telecom, water)	Tropical Depressions
Bombs/ Improvised Explosive Device (IED) Terrorism	Medical Emergency	Data Breach	Urban fire	Tornadoes and Severe Thunderstorms
Pandemic/ Epidemic	Public Health Incident		Public Health Emergencies	High Winds
Cyber/IT Disruption	Structure fire/ Arson			Flooding
	Threat of harm/ Criminal Activity			Snow and Ice Storms
	Severe Weather/ Tornado			Civil Disturbance
	Winter Storm			Bomb Threats
				Terrorist attack – Bombing
				Weapons of Mass Destruction incident
				Assault
				Robbery
				Shootings
				Kidnappings
				Hostage Barricade

Figure 11.1. List of Annexes or Appendices of Potential Threats and Hazards in Selected Operational Safety Plans/Institutions

operations for each particular type of emergency. This Team utilizes the Incident Command System (ICS), which designates an Incident Commander (IC) who leads the assembled supporting IMT members (experts). These experts are the leads for a coalition of internal and external partners relevant to their particular area of expertise.

When interviewing the ISU (2020) representative, he shared that:

> So whether you have the fire department comes out and shows them how to use a fire extinguisher, CPR training, you have a person come in and talk about environmental health and safety . . . they need to have the basic ICS training and then there needs to be training for our campus. How you are going to do things on your campus, who are the people who are contacting, not by name, but by title and who are our external partners and make sure you develop a strong relationship with your local, state, and federal partners for emergency management. You'll be surprised at how they will tell you about grants opportunities, be willing to sponsor training programs on your campus. This brings people to your campus and it brings experts to your campus and that's the networking part of it. So you have to have a total of community engagement internally and externally.

When having a plan, it is important, according to the EVMS (2020) representative to ensure that,

> . . . the plan is adaptable and that's a good thing with NIMS and ICS; the plans are adaptable . . . in my experience from Norfolk being in strategic management and writing up policies and procedures, it never failed. You'll write up a policy, you send it down to the assistant chiefs and captain, they all say that looks good. You put it out and the office that has been on one year finds the big mistake. . . . So make sure that it gets examined, practiced, and looked at various levels to make sure that it will work. Not just theoretically, but that it will work . . . if you can catch some of those things before the event then you might save yourself some time some property and a life or something so that part of it and like I say practice it and then be aware that nobody's campus stays the same. Nobody's area stays the same; it's constantly changing and that you have to be ready and willing to review it and when changes occur, to be sure to implement or add those or look at how that plan now impacts . . .

TCC's (2020) representative also commented on what he believed would be a "best practice," sharing:

> I think it's getting multiple stakeholders at the table as you're doing a plan cause you know just the public safety folks alone developing a plan it's too much of a vacuum and you got a narrow set of . . . you know you're only in a certain environment at whatever institution that you're at. I think knowing the needs

and the worries of students, faculty, and staff, the public, it's just so many people involved that come onto the college campus. I really think you have to get a working group so they can understand and provide you with the input that you can put in that plan.

Lastly, the NASA (2020) representative shared his thought about "best practices" and recommendations for others,

> Well, depending on what it would be I would have to, first of all I would have to stay within my expertise or whatever review their plan to see how they do it. Like I said, when I first got here I didn't sit down and look at the plan for a spill. I didn't even know they had hazardous chemicals out here [Langley], you know. Kennedy, we were around them all the time with the shuttle at the launch pads. It wasn't, you know, it was not unusual to see a puff of orange or rusty color smoke coming your way and that stuff will kill you when you smell it. So you know so I didn't know what they had here [Langley] so I didn't really sit and look at their plans on how you would handle a hazardous spill or whatever. I still haven't to be quite honest with you. I have a certain [pause] well my guys have a certain little piece of that pie when that happens they do this everybody else does other things. Just like active shooter. We do a certain part of that whole pie. Outside agencies come in, sets up a wash area in case somebody is contaminated and they have to get washed down. The problem with something like that is that massive you have so many people involved in it and if they don't work together, and what I saw when I first got here, people were stepping on each other toes saying "I'm the boss, I'm the boss, I'm the boss." You got someone over there that might have been you know contaminated by something, I don't care who the boss is you guys have plans, get it done. I don't care who it is. If you want pats on the back and "look what I did" wait until after the situation is done. Then I'll come over there and pat you on the back if that's what you need, you know.

The purpose of Research Question #3 was to determine candidate "best practices" utilized by the five college-affiliated institutions. Document analysis of the operational safety plans and emergency management personnel interviews generated five potential "best practices." Best Practice #1, Training, should be conducted annually with tabletop or full-scale exercises that simulate a potential emergency event. This candidate "best practice" aligned with the Training and Emergency Management protocol themes. Best Practice #2, Institution's Operational Safety Plan Review, refers to emergency managers implementing an annual review process for maintaining their operational safety plans as current and enhancing them as needed. This candidate "best practice" aligned with the Communication, Coordination, Resources, and Emergency Management protocol themes. Best Practice #3, External Resources, refers to the utilization of resources (e.g., NIMS,

EMAP, FEMA, etc.) by all five institutions in guiding their operational safety plan in design and implementation. This candidate "best practice" aligned with the Resources and Emergency Management themes. Best Practice #4, Response Framework, discussed how the five institutions utilized annexes, appendices, or both that provided guidelines when preparing, responding, or from a crisis via natural, manmade, or technological. This candidate "best practice" aligned with the Communication, Coordination, and Emergency Management themes. Best Practice #5, Leverage Intellectual Assets, refers to how all five institutions defined their Emergency Operation Center (EOC) and instructions for activating, staffing, and operating in response to a crisis (i.e., before, during, and after). Furthermore, it relies on input from internal and external experts for operational safety plan design review. This candidate "best practice" aligned with Emergency Threat, Coordination, Communication, Resources, and Emergency Management themes.

Chapter Twelve

Investigative Outcomes

Until Hurricane Katrina in 2005 and the 2007 Virginia Tech massacre, there were few studies examining "best practices" for operational safety plan development on college and university campuses in preparation for natural and manmade crises. In fact, the field primarily focused on aspects of active shooter events and emergency planning for their prevention at K–12 institutions (Blair, Nichols, Burns, & Curnutt, 2013; Bonanno & Levenson, 2014; EveryTown, 2018; Fox & Savage, 2009). Furthermore, the term "operational safety plan" did not exist until 2007, although higher education institutions did have some form of emergency management plans (Asmussen & Creswell, 2013; Bonanno & Levenson, 2014; Hughes, White, & Hertz, 2008; NCCPS, 2016b; NLECTC, 2009). As emergencies have occurred (and will continue to occur), they have exposed weaknesses in institutions' operational safety planning processes, which were addressed in a reactive manner in the aftermath of a crisis (Cowen & Seifter, 2018; Cooper & Block, 2006; DHS, 2006; Johnson & Rainey, 2007; van Heerden & Bryan, 2006). Events like September 11, Hurricane Katrina, and Virginia Tech have provided ". . . the possibility of transformation, both as a strategy for survival and as a way to reset the university" (Cowen and Seifter, 2018, pp. 6–7).

In the wake of Virginia Tech, research primarily focused on aspects of responding to criminal (i.e., manmade) incidents at colleges and universities, including stakeholders' perceptions of campus safety (Hughes, White, & Hertz, 2008; Jennings, Gover, & Pudrzynska, 2007; Lannon, 2014; Shafer, Heiple, Giblin, & Burruss, 2010; Thompson et al., 2009; Zugazaga, Werner, Clifford, Weaver, & Ware, 2016). Several subsequent studies also examined how to more effectively manage communications (Sheldon 2018; Traynor, 2012; Zugazaga et al., 2016). Lastly, researchers concluded that when training for crises is provided (i.e., lectures, mock scenarios, videos, etc.) participants perceived themselves as better prepared to survive an incident (Cowen &

Seifter, 2018; Ford & Frei, 2016, Harrison, 2014). Altogether, the research literature provided insight when developing six protocol themes, which aided in the identification of the following guiding principles, implementation factors, and candidate "best practices" that can enhance the design and implementation of operational safety plans if adopted (Blair & Martaindale; 2013; Blair, Nichols, Burns, & Curnutt, 2013; Blair & Schweit, 2014).

GUIDING DESIGN PRINCIPLES

Build Strong Relationships (Guiding Principle #1)

This premise is to invite internal and external (i.e., local, state, and federal entities) experts in assisting with the overall design of an institution's operational safety plan. External first responders regardless of affiliation can support an institution during the preparation, mitigation, and recovery from a major disaster. By partnering with external experts (i.e., "building the relationship"), senior administrators learn what training, equipment, and resources are actually available to their institutions (Bauman, 2017; GAO, 2018).

Higher education institutions commonly utilize federal external expertise through the National Incident Management System (NIMS) for the design and implementation of their operational safety plans, a behavior consistent with loosely coupled and Open Systems Theory (FEMA, 2011b; GAO, 2018; Lawrence & Lorsch, 1967; Scott & Davis, 2007). All five institutions utilized NIMS in their operational safety plan, including the Incident Command System (ICS), even though a representative from Idaho State University [ISU] stated that,

> . . . I've always felt that ICS is cumbersome, it's good for maybe certain situations, but in this [COVID-19] case we needed to make decisions quickly . . . I say this because oftentimes, strict ICS adherence does not lend itself to every situation and needs to be modified. What I have seen happen is that the responders are going through extra steps to complete all the forms and fill as many of the positions as possible instead of modifying ICS to meet their needs by following the most applicable ICS concepts. (ISU, 2020)

The current study supports the findings of Becker (2004, 2010) and Veenema, Walden, Feinstein, and Williams (2008) who found that emergency planners seek input and feedback not only from within the institution, but also from external resource entities in order to bolster their operational safety plans and build relationships. The five college-affiliated institutions studied here leveraged multiple relationships of specialized expertise within their hierarchical and complex environments (Scott & Davis, 2007).

The ODU representative (2020) concurred, saying that he and his team assemble subject matter experts and solicit their feedback in order to capture their knowledge and develop a more effective operational safety plan. As Mason (2014) stated, ". . . I had the wisdom, and some good fortune, to find the best people, coordinate and decide when needed, but mostly to get out of the way and let talented people do their jobs" (p. 73).

Know Your Environmental Hazards (Guiding Principle #2)

Under this principle, each institution identifies specific natural, technological, or manmade threats to their college or university by using some type of risk assessment tool. In the case of ISU, they utilized a Threat Hazard Identification Risk Assessment (THIRA) survey along with a committee board. This method allowed emergency managers to enhance their operational safety plans such that the most likely disasters are on their preparation list. By contrast, all Virginia institutions are now mandated to create, among other things, threat assessment teams (legislative Code of Virginia 23-9.2:10 [effective March 7, 2008] and 23.1-805 [effective October 1, 2016]). These units assess whether an individual is either a threat to him or herself or to others, and then connect them with resources in order to prevent a potential crisis (Evans, Bira, Gastelum, Weiss, & Vanderford, 2018; Lannon, 2014; Randazzo & Plummer, 2009). The current study supported the findings of several studies whose authors found that, when implementing an institution- or individual-level threat assessment method, emergency managers were able to more effectively address potential disasters (before, during, and after) whether they were natural, technological, or manmade (Blair & Martaindale; 2013; Evans, Bira, Gastelum, Weiss, & Vanderford, 2018; Fox & Savage, 2009; Lannon, 2014; Randazzo & Plummer, 2009). Additionally, identifying potential threats afford emergency managers the opportunity to then gather necessary resources and allocate them appropriately.

A lack of preparation and coordination can cost higher education institutions millions of dollars in damages as well as long-term losses in student enrollment and faculty employment (Cooper & Block, 2006; Cowen & Seifter, 2018; Johnson & Rainey, 2007). For example, when Hurricane Katrina struck New Orleans, it nearly destroyed

> . . . the university and causing damage to Tulane that amounted to $650 million. I won't repeat all the details of the Renewal Plan we constructed to save the university, but the basics involved merging seven undergraduate colleges into one, eliminating several undergraduate and graduate programs, downsizing the medical school, suspending half the athletic programs, and ultimately letting go about eight hundred of our full-time faculty and staff. (Cowen & Seifter, 2018)

Operational Safety Plan Enhancement (Guiding Principle #3)

This particular principle dealt with procedural enhancement, based on "lessons learned," since hazardous event responses require constant improvement (FEMA, 2011a; FEMA 2011b; FEMA, 2012; Waugh, 2004). In addition, this allows emergency planners to address hazards not yet experienced (e.g., Covid-19). Institutions in this study achieved this guiding principle in a number of different ways. For example, ISU (2019) and ODU (2019) created an after action review process (After Action Reports/Improvement Plans [AARs/IPs]), what ODU refers to as a "Hot Wash" (ODU, 2019, p. A-12). The studied institutions outlined procedures that evaluated participants and agencies after a training exercise or an actual emergency event, which were "... essential for identifying issues that need correction or capturing improvised approaches that may be applicable for future incidents/emergencies/events" (ODU, 2019, p. 52). These data were consistent with the analytical procedures and findings reported by several authors (Asmussen & Creswell, 2013; Briggs & Kennedy, 2016; Cooper & Block, 2006; Ford & Frei, 2016; Fox & Savage, 2009; Mason, 2014; Nelson, 2014; Sheldon, 2018; Stafford, 2014; Virginia Tech Review Panel, 2007). For example, Asmussen and Creswell's (2013) whole rationale for conducting their qualitative study was to understand what happened and then to make recommendations on how to handle an active shooter event in the future. Another representative example was that of Fox and Savage (2009), who reviewed taskforce recommendations for their applicability to higher education institutions and proposed additional improvements. Lastly, according to Stafford (2014),

> Campuses refer to tabletop exercise and practices, but many of them do not actually exercise the emergency response plan. This has always been important, but it has not necessarily been a priority at many colleges and universities. ... It is imperative to exercise the plan so that all readers on campus understand their role during an emergency, and the campus can continue to enhance the plan as participants learn what has not been addressed in an exercise environment, rather than when the real emergency happens on the campus. Campuses must make sure that the emergency response ... plans are not just "good in theory" but that they work in practice. (p. 52)

SUCCESSFUL IMPLEMENTATION FACTORS

Political/Legal Factors (Implementation Factor #1)

All five institutions depended on their general counsel for guidance and final approval of their operational safety plan. This was especially true for the

Virginia institutions, which have to comply with Virginia state code 23.1-804 (which also complies with federal law) that stipulates an emergency operational safety plan. Furthermore, these higher education institutions also had to conform to both Title IX (1972) and Clery Act of 1990 by reporting any criminal activity in an annual report (Lipka, 2007; Mahaffie, 2014; Mumper et al., 2016). To illustrate, an ODU (2020) representative stated that, ". . . we vetted the plan [CEMP] through the office of general counsel and make sure they were happy with it. . . . We are thinking about things like Clery compliance. That's going to be one of the biggest ones and that's the notification. . . ." The current study supported the findings of Baker and Boland (2011), Gregory and Janosik (2002), and Janosik and Gregory (2003), which included data regarding awareness of and compliance with the Clery Act as a component to improving campus safety. Janosik and Gregory (2003) reported that campus law enforcement were surveyed to determine their awareness of the Clery Act (all indicated knowledge of it), and 43 percent agreed that compliance would improve campus safety. As part of this compliance requirement, many higher education institutions, including the ones studied here, have installed their own safety measures (e.g., camera/security systems, etc.) to keep their campus community safe (Baker & Boland, 2011; Gregory & Janosik, 2002).

However, as of October 2020, the U.S. Department of Education rescinded the 2016 Clery Handbook, which means that every institution in the country may need to rethink their Clery-based approach, especially since the 2020 election outcome will likely change the politics of the Clery handbook yet again. The current study's institutions were also not immune to national or administrative personnel politics; in fact, political factors were the impetus for indefinite postponement of commissioning a police force at TCC (2020) due to the COVID-19 pandemic and police brutality movement. This is consistent with numerous published studies (Bauman, 2017; Eckel, 2015; GAO, 2018; Randazzo & Cameron, 2012; Randazzo & Plummer, 2009; Richardson, 1994 Theodoulou & Kofinis, 2004). To illustrate, in the wake of the Virginia Tech massacre, the Virginia Tech Panel Report (2007) captured the changing political environment that allowed for passage of the legal mandate for operational safety plans.

Financial Factors (Implementation Factor #2)

This factor was ubiquitous among the appendices or annexes of the five institutions' operational safety plans. One of the most common references to financial factors was how to determine resource allocation during and after crisis situations. Specifically, ODU's (2019) ESF 7 outlined a list of suppliers to expedite resource procurement during a crisis. This finding supports literature documenting methods the federal government uses when allocating resources and equipment (Bauman, 2017; Cooper & Block, 2006; Dow & Cutter, 2000; FEMA, 2011b; Kealy, 2003; Kraska, 2007; Waugh, 2003). In the absence of well-defined procedures, there can be miscommunication and outright failure to meet emergency needs as documented in Cooper and Block (2006) following Hurricane Katrina's landfall. Colleges and universities, who have also lacked clear guidelines, have faced lawsuits and financial settlements with victims (Blanchard & Baez, 2016; Johnson, 2012; Lipka, 2007; Lipka, 2008; Randazzo & Plummer, 2009; U.S. Department of Education, 2007; Virginia Tech Panel Report, 2007).

Lastly, higher education emergency managers at the five institutions in this study utilized their financial resources to recruit subject matter experts in order to obtain benefits in operational safety plan development. To illustrate, ODU (2020) representatives submitted grant proposals in order to obtain funds for recruiting experts to the college, which normally costs tens of thousands of dollars. In addition, he stated it costs five to ten thousand dollars in order to obtain an EMAP certification like the one held by Idaho State University (ODU, 2020). However, this study found that the four Virginia institutions struggled with obtaining funds necessary to purchase emergency equipment and resources they deemed essential. This was in contrast with Idaho State University where the interviewee stated that "There were no financial challenges. We did not have to sacrifice anything to get something we felt was important. Our institution provided the funding that was necessary" (ISU, 2020).

Operational Factors (Implementation Factor #3)

Data analysis identified two issues, an Emergency Operations Center (EOC) and membership on an institution's incident management team, as salient to successful implementation of its operational safety plan. All five of the institutions designated a primary and secondary EOC to handle any natural or manmade incident responses, which are consistent with guidelines established by the federal National Incident Management System (NIMS). Furthermore, the institution's utilization of an incident management system (ICS) to select its incident management team during operational safety plan implementation supports Waugh (2004), who affirmed that the, "ICS was designed to coordinate multi-organizational responses to wildfires and has been adapted to other kinds of incidents . . . a system for managing resources" (p. 384). Lastly, Oliver (2009) indicated that, "ICS is a management system designed for use with multiple agencies from the same sector (e.g., all police), or multiple agencies from across sectors (e.g., police, fire, etc.), to manage large scale events, terrorist attacks, or natural disasters . . ." (p. 255).

Others Factors to Consider (Implementation Factor #4)

This factor took into account an organization's culture and environment when implementing its operational safety plan. All five institutions had varying geographic locations, mission statements, or culture environments. To illustrate, ODU's (2018e, 2019) geographic location in an urban coastal environment and its research II designation placed this university in a distinct leadership role with regards to development of mitigation strategies for sea level rise and climate change. This observation along with others supports Myers and Lusk (2017), Lawrence and Lorsch (1967), and Weick (1976), who reported that differences in environment (e.g., geographical location) would impact organizations (e.g., college-affiliated institutions) and their cultures differently, resulting in different outcomes (e.g., operational safety plans). This study's findings also support the work of authors looking at the role of presidents and senior administrators, and how their support (or lack thereof) of their institution's emergency support personnel influences where resources, equipment, etc. are distributed during and after a crisis (i.e., what is important to the organizational culture) (Asmussen & Creswell, 2013; Cowen & Seifter, 2018; Johnson & Rainey, 2007; Richardson, 1994; Stripling, 2019; van Heerden & Bryan, 2006).

OPERATIONAL SAFETY PLAN "BEST PRACTICES"

Training (Best Practice #1)

Training was intended to meet the following objectives: preventing, mitigating, preparing, responding, and recovering for various types of emergencies. All institutions studied here utilized some type of training regimen, which included training courses, tabletop exercises, and full-scale mock scenarios to ensure readiness for responding to an actual natural or manmade disaster. The benefit of this training is to assist in reducing and mitigating risk, which supports what previous researchers have found (Blair & Martaindale, 2013; Blair, Nichols, Burns, & Curnutt, 2013; Briggs & Kennedy, 2016; Cowen & Seifter, 2018; Harrison, 2014; NCCPS, 2016b; NDPC, 2018; Schafer, Heiple, Giblin, & Burruss, 2010). Both Cowen and Seifter (2018) and Harrison (2014) highlighted the importance of training as many times as possible with realistic scenarios and equipment in order to maximize the effectiveness of an organization's emergency response.

However, analyses in the current study revealed that training was not a major priority relative to the other protocol themes. When examining coding frequencies of the Training protocol theme, all five institutions' results fell within a range of only 3–7%. Although ISU (i.e., the blue light institution) stated "Training" in its operational safety plan documents 7 percent of the time, the ISU (2020) representative revealed a much more extensive commitment to "training" by mentioning that they conduct training meetings monthly. This finding is consistent with the published EMAP (2019) Standards which outlined a training, assessment, development, and implementation process for institutions to obtain and maintain their certification. An institution's training procedure should include: 1) a training program that addresses identified hazards, 2) a training assessment instrument, 3) training that is conducted regularly based on internal and external objectives, 4) training that is consistent with personnel's current responsibilities, 5) records that are maintained about the types of training exercises completed and who participated, and 6) a method to evaluate and revise this training process (EMAP, 2019). Furthermore, this study's findings also match with what Ford and Frei (2016) report; that is, a training video increased participants' perception of their preparedness for an active shooter event, which supported objectives 1, 3, and 4 of the EMAP (2019) training standard. One last finding from this study, the importance of training first responders and campus stakeholders, supports Blair and Martaindale (2013), Briggs and Kennedy (2016), and Sheldon (2018), who all reported advantages of training first responders that included, among other things, strengthening their ability to be ready for a potential fight, be trained in IED usage, and be prepared to provide medical care for victims at a crisis.

Institution's Operational Safety Plan Review (Best Practice #2)

All five studied institutions conducted an annual assessment of their operational safety plans, which includes supplemental plans such as annexes and appendices. For the Virginia institutions, personnel were guided by the code of Virginia (§23.1-804). The ODU (2020) representative stated that they review their plan annually to ensure that it reflects their mission and it is not just a plan handed over from another institution. He further stated they have an after action review process in which the emergency team meets and discusses ". . . what went well and what didn't" (ODU, 2020) and then this data is available to guide any needed changes or updates to their operational safety plan. These findings are consistent with FEMA's (2015) post-disaster framework that operational safety plan managers utilize to assess and evaluate, identify needed resources, and to exercise flexibility in their operations. In this current study, the "best practice" in reviewing an operational safety plan annually supports Stafford (2014) in which the author discussed how institutions' emergency teams review their operational safety plans to enhance or update their documents during or after a crisis in order to continue to keep the campus community safe. In addition, this study's "best practice" also confirms the findings of Mason (2014), who argued that being flexible, making enhancements to an institution's (flood) crisis response when needed, and increasing resource availability would provide an emergency response team with the tools to decrease the potential for wasted time and effort when responding to a future crisis.

External Resources (Best Practice #3)

Emergency managers at the five institutions studied here incorporated as many resource standards (from NIMS, EMAP, FEMA, OSHA, SCHEV, etc.) as possible to remain in compliance when designing and implementing operational safety plans. With ISU becoming the second institution in the United States to receive the EMAP certification, ISU's (2020) representative stated his team welcomes any information regarding methods for constantly improving their operational safety plan, including sources with a specific application to higher education. He further emphasized the importance of external resources with:

> . . . local, state, and federal partners for emergency management. You'll be surprised at how they will tell you about grants opportunities, willing to sponsor training programs on your campus. This brings people to your campus and it brings experts to your campus and that's the networking part of it so you have . . . a total of community engagement . . . (ISU, 2020)

This natural information-seeking behavior observed in the current study supports findings previously published (Asmussen & Creswell, 2013; Johnson & Rainey, 2007; Nelson, 2014; Randazzo & Cameron, 2012; Randazzo & Plummer, 2009; van Heerden & Bryan, 2006; VA Tech Review Panel, 2007). For example, students at the University of Nebraska-Lincoln sought external resources on how to remain safe in the aftermath of an active shooter (Asmussen & Creswell, 2013). Additionally, Blair and Martaindale (2013) provided data from previous active shooter events that could then inform strategies for training and equipment procurement. Such a data-driven approach would be most helpful as emergency managers construct their operational safety plans with the most up-to-date information before natural and manmade disasters strike. Unfortunately, research also showed that most emergency managers do not seek this information proactively, but rather reactively in response to a crisis (Asmussen & Creswell, 2013; Randazzo & Plummer, 2009; VA Tech Review Panel, 2007).

Response Framework (Best Practice #4)

As a part of their response frameworks, the five studied institutions listed their potential threats in their operational safety plans; that is, they incorporated annexes, appendices, or both for every potential threat with specific directions on preparing for, responding to, and recovering from these natural, technological, or manmade crises. This study's candidate "best practice" partially contradicts what can be found in the literature as many researchers report chaos in the absence of such a step-by-step set of directions and guidelines specific to each crime or natural disaster (Donald, 2009; Dow & Cutter, 2000; Criminal Justice, 2019; Cornish & Clarke, 1986; Ford & Frei, 2016; Gleick, 2008; Grasmick & Bursik, 1990; Poole, 2009; Sheldon, 2018). The premise can best be illustrated by the 2005 Hurricane Katrina event and the 2007 mass shooting at Virginia Tech. When Hurricane Katrina hit New Orleans, it exposed many weaknesses in the emergency management plan, including the dire consequences of not detailing how DHS would supplement water and ice needs in areas identified as most needy by the 2004 Hurricane Pam simulation (Cooper & Block, 2006). Meanwhile, due to a lack of an emergency plan at Virginia Tech, emergency managers did not communicate effectively the potential danger following their discovery of the shooter's first two victims, which created chaos when the shooter returned to campus (Virginia Tech Review Panel, 2007). If higher education administrators and emergency managers in these situations have well-developed response frameworks, it will mitigate property damage and save lives (Asmussen & Creswell, 2013; Cowen & Seifter, 2018; Fox & Savage, 2009; Harrison, 2014; International Association of Emergency Managers [IAEM], 2007; Mason, 2014; Nelson, 2014; Sheldon, 2018; Stafford, 2014; Thompson et al., 2009; Traynor, 2012; Virginia Tech Review Panel, 2007; Waugh, 2003).

Leverage Intellectual Assets (Best Practice #5)

Representatives of the five colleges, universities, and affiliates noted that they designated subject matter experts (internally and externally) when forming an incident management team, which oversaw a crisis from onset to completion. Like his peers, the NASA (2020) representative also affirmed the importance of individuals' expertise when designing and implementing an effective operational safety plan. Once the team is assembled, representatives from all the studied institutions stated that an Incident Commander (IC) would be appointed to coordinate experts and to deploy them where they are needed most so as to maximize chances for a successful response. The premise of "Leverage Intellectual Assets," which involves recruiting experts in the field for their intellectual knowledge to help strengthen and bolster an operational response, supports the findings from numerous studies (Becker, 2004; Monahan, 2010; Vervaele, 2005). For example, Vervaele (2005) and Monahan (2010) argued that fusion centers (i.e., intelligence-led policing), which are designed for "conducting 'threat assessments' for events and linking 'suspicious activities reports' to other data to create profiles of individuals or groups" (p. 84), serve as a valuable resource in keeping people safe. Finally, in his qualitative study about emergency communication during a fictional terrorist attack, Becker (2004) concluded that information sharing is paramount for emergency personnel.

> Professionals described information as crucial, both to carry out professional duties and to reduce the overall terror of the situation. In a typical comment, one health-care professional explained: "I think information is essential for us, but it's also essential for us to try to control the terror and the havoc, for us to give other people the calming that we would need to deal. We would need to have as much information as we could possibly acquire." (p. 203)

Central to information sharing is the premise that the subject matter experts be reliable (i.e., "Trust, but verify" —Ronald Reagan). Had the experts been able to share quality information across functional units within the college community at Virginia Tech, there might very well have been a different outcome (Randazzo & Plummer, 2007; Virginia Tech Panel Report). To illustrate, in the months leading up to April 16, 2007, mental health professionals, professors, and even campus police became aware of Cho's stalking and suicidal tendencies, yet legal constraints and campus cultural norms prevented these individuals from sharing their knowledge with others (Randazzo & Plummer, 2007; Virginia Tech Panel Report). As recently as 2018, the U.S. Government Accountability Office (GAO) reported that higher education emergency personnel were not aware of all the intellectual assets available from the federal government for operational safety planning, triggering a recommendation for better information sharing practices to remedy this deficiency.

Chapter Thirteen

Implications for Design and Implementation

There were a number of practical and theoretical implications that stemmed from the results of this multiple case study research. Document analysis as well as interview data suggested how operational safety plan practice could advance in design and implementation. Higher education institutions utilize operational safety plans to reduce liability, protect their property, and keep members of their campus community safe. Thus, studying these operational safety plans have important ramifications for enhancing both the research field's knowledge of what constitutes "best practices" for these documents as well as application of these principles by emergency managers in the field. Finally, this study revealed several gaps and limitations that provide suggestions for future research that would advance the understanding of operational safety planning for colleges, universities, and their affiliates.

PRACTICAL IMPLICATIONS

Upon review of the available research, a document analysis protocol was derived from the literature, proposing six themes that guided the research in this study that identified guiding principles, implementation factors, and candidate "best practices" for the design and implementation of operational safety plans (Asmussen & Creswell, 2013; Bauman, 2017; Blair & Martaindale, 2013; Dahl, Bonham, & Reddington, 2016; Inskeep, 2019; NCCPS, 2016b; Rasmussen, 2019; Thompson, Price, Mrdjenovich, & Khubchandani, 2009). For the purpose of this study, practical implications of these six protocol themes (i.e., Training, Emergency Threat, Resources, Communication, Coordination, and Emergency Management) were grouped as follows: Preparation and Response. When examining previous studies, it was noted that both components, Preparation and Response, were generally treated with equal importance when it came to operational safety planning (Bataille & Cordova, 2014; Booker, 2014; Cooper & Block, 2006; FEMA, 2011a; FEMA, 2011b; Ford & Frei, 2016).

Under the Preparation category, the Training and Emergency Threat protocol themes captured those activities that an institution would engage in before the onset of an emergency. In fact, several operational safety plans analyzed here contained a schematic or a written description of the framework guiding design and implementation of their operational safety plans (ODU, 2019; TCC, 2017; EVMS, 2017). These frameworks each described five components, "prevent, mitigate against, prepare for, respond to, and recover from an emergency . . ." (ODU, 2019, pp. 1, 13, 15, 21). Using ODU as a representative example, these five parts are drawn in such a way as to imply that all are to be treated as equals (see the reprinted ODU framework schematic in figure 13.1).

However, data revealed that these Preparation components were not treated equally when compared to the Response category (e.g., Training appeared in 3–7 percent of all the codes while Emergency Threat appeared in 6–8 percent of all the codes). Practically speaking, these results revealed

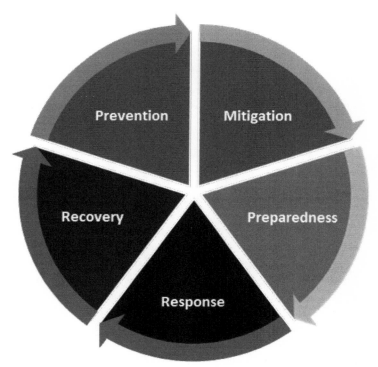

Figure 13.1.   Old Dominion University's Emergency Management Cycle

that an institution is likely to be less than completely prepared to implement their operational safety plan during moments of crisis. Although it was beyond the scope of this project, the following incident confirmed this practical implication. In the summer of 2017, an institution experienced a near fatal attack on campus when a student followed a professor into a restroom where the assailant pointed a gun at the victim's head and demanded that they not scream. Naturally, the victim screamed and darted out of the restroom. An unpublished analysis by this author revealed that senior administrators and first responders did not effectively communicate with each other and the campus community due to a lack of sufficient Training (e.g., deans did not know how to operate the emergency phone alert feature), which caused unnecessary chaos and demonstrated the institution was not prepared for an Emergency Threat of this magnitude. By contrast, while the blue light institution, ISU, also had unequal references to Training (7%) and to Emergency Threat (8%) relative to the emphasis given to other Response protocol themes in its operational safety plan, the ISU (2020) representative discussed at length though not only the importance of Training to his team's preparation, but also the monthly Training sessions that his team enthusiastically participated in. Although the author was not aware of any recent emergency incidents at this particular blue light institution, the practical implication of this emergency manager's investment in his team's training and preparation increases the likelihood that they will implement a successful response to a future crisis situation. Therefore, in day-to-day operations, it is recommended that an institution's emergency management team gives as much weight to the Preparation aspects of operational safety planning as they do to the Response to a natural or manmade disaster.

Results obtained from the current study emphasize the adage, "you play like you practice" (Luttrell & Wasserman, 2014). Extrapolating back to the research literature, it has been documented that prior to Hurricane Katrina making landfall in August 2005, New Orleans and Louisiana officials squandered federal and local resources that were earmarked for safeguarding the region from disastrous effects of flooding (Cooper & Block, 2006). Furthermore, a lack of in-depth Preparation at a 2004 DHS-funded simulation exercise exacerbated what eventually unfolded in the actual Response. For example, local emergency managers calculated that "1.53 million gallons of water and 5.5 million pounds of ice to the area each day" (Cooper & Block, 2006, p. 19) were needed in an event of a real hurricane. However, when Hurricane Katrina actually happened, the federal government could not deliver the resources needed as promised regardless of whether they were basic items (e.g., flashlights, water, ice, etc.) or more advanced equipment such as mobile communication centers (Cooper & Block, 2006). Had these emergency managers placed more effort into the Preparation portion of operational safety planning for this and other crisis incidents, it is reasonable to conclude that the Response would have been much more effective at mitigating negative impacts of disasters (Briggs & Kennedy, 2016; Cooper & Block, 2006; Cowen & Seifter, 2018; Dow & Cutter, 2000; Ford & Frei, 2016; Tonry & Farrington, 1995; Waugh, 2003).

Another practical implication to follow from the results obtained here is the salience of soliciting and capturing the knowledge of an assembled team of experts (including in-house stakeholders) during every phase of operational safety plan design and implementation. In each institution's document analysis, it was revealed that the college's or university's emergency manager assembled an emergency management team when activating the Emergency Operations Center (EOC), which included individuals whose roles and expertise assist with the particular emergency in progress (EVMS, 2017; ISU, 2019; NASA, 2015; ODU, 2019; TCC, 2017). So, while the institution applied its intellectual assets during a Response, it was less obvious from document analysis alone how often these experts were leveraged on a regular basis during overall operational safety plan maintenance during Preparation phases (EVMS, 2017; ODU, 2019; NASA, 2015; TCC, 2017). Aside from ISU, emergency managers interviewed for this study did not explicitly address their procedures for incorporating expert knowledge on a regular basis beyond crisis response, a prescribed annual review, and an annual training exercise (EVMS, 2017; ODU, 2019; NASA, 2015; TCC, 2017). This raises the issues of 1) how do institutions become aware of the latest research findings regarding "best practices" for operational safety planning, and then 2) how do they incorporate those findings in order to enhance their plans for future use (GAO, 2018).

One of the most striking features of ISU's (2019, 2020) approach to operational safety planning was its supportive institutional culture that encourages monthly meetings for the purpose of disseminating current crisis management knowledge, research findings, and strategies through discussion and training irrespective of an in-progress emergency. In doing so, the ISU emergency manager, along with the university President, has created a collegial environment in which these established personal relationships flourish, increasing the chances for a more successful response to an actual crisis (Waugh, 2004). The ISU (2020) representative discussed at length the importance of not only staying up-to-date on NIMS and ICS resources, but also examining other sources of knowledge to include, not limited to, research studies and documents from the National Center for Campus Public Safety (NCCPS), the Readiness and Emergency Management for Schools Technical Assistance Center (REMS TA Center), and the Disaster Resilient Universities (DRU) Listserv provided by the University of Oregon. As this study's blue light institution, Idaho State

University engages in this kind of continual learning behavior with experts for operational safety plan enhancement in part because the Emergency Management Accreditation Program (EMAP) certification process dictates that such a behavior be an integral part of maintaining accreditation. EMAP (2019) assists higher education institutions and agencies with constructing a comprehensive operational safety plan that meets their needs, beginning with a unique mission statement, plan objectives, implementation methods, and a continual maintenance process, which includes constant evaluation and revision. The approach that ISU has taken with its experts and operational safety plan, reinforced by its EMAP certification status, results in a "living" document, which the institution's emergency management team has a stronger "relationship" with as a result of multiple periodic interactions throughout each calendar year. This perspective is in stark contrast to that taken at other institutions where most plans ". . . sit unread in disaster offices . . . the collection of disaster plans on . . . [the] bookshelf stretches for several feet" (Cooper & Block, 2006, p. 5).

Having an operational safety plan for natural and manmade disasters provides the equivalent of a roadmap and GPS device in guiding an institution through a crisis. Data obtained in this study implied that institutions benefit when they have external guidance (i.e., a roadmap and framework) for designing and implementing their operational safety plans (i.e., the roadmap and GPS to navigate a crisis). In every institution's operational safety plan, emergency personnel acknowledged using FEMA's National Incident Management System (NIMS) and Incident Command System (ICS) as their foundational framework in order to ". . . prevent, mitigate against, prepare for, respond to, and recover from an emergency . . ." (FEMA, 2011a; FEMA, 2011b; FEMA, 2012; FEMA, 2015). However, it became clear through review of the literature as well as data analysis that there are additional frameworks available to supplement the NIMS and ICS guidelines (DHS, 2018; EMAP, 2019; GAO, 2018; IAEM, 2007; NCCPS, 2016a; NCCPS, 2016b). As mentioned previously, the ISU team utilized a wide array of research and resources, not the least of which is their EMAP accreditation. The Standards put forth by EMAP (2019) provide a clear set of guidelines (i.e., roadmap) that allow emergency management and their stakeholders to conceptualize organizational planning and implementation strategies from both Bottom-Up and Top-Down approaches. While initial EMAP accreditation indicates that an institution has met the minimum set forth in the Standards, it is expected that emergency managers will exceed these basic requirements by engaging in constant enhancement of their procedures for training, coordination and identification of specific personnel responsibilities, institutional preparedness, and recovery from all natural and manmade hazards that could potentially threaten the college or university (EMAP, 2019). This premise is not unlike that of a police academy's basic training program, which certifies law enforcement officers as meeting the minimum standards set by the Department of Criminal Justice Services (DCJS), and in-service recertification school that is required of an officer if they wish to continue and advance in their careers (DCJS, 2020).

The EMAP (2019) Standards framework establishes not only a checkbox for a cursory review each year (short-term), but also outlines a multi-year strategic roadmap that helps to strengthen an institution's goals, milestones, and financial resources with respect to the operational safety plan beyond any one crisis (long-term). By defining various elements (e.g., identification of relevant personnel, tasks, and rationale) needed for an effective operational safety plan in both the short-term and long-term, an institution makes the case for a compelling emergency management strategic plan across the coming year, the next five years, and even ten years into the future (EMAP, 2019). As an analogy, certain elements must be present and proven beyond a reasonable doubt in order to convict someone of a crime. In the short-term, a police officer must establish facts and circumstances for probable cause, which leads to an arrest (Bouffard & Exum, 2013; Cornish & Clarke, 1986; Grasmick & Bursik, 1990). Then, in the long-term, these elements are taken by prosecutors to compellingly convince the court of the suspect's guilt (Bouffard & Exum, 2013; Criminal Justice, 2019; Cornish & Clarke, 1986; Grasmick & Bursik, 1990; Kubrin, Stucky, & Krohn, 2009).

Under EMAP's (2019) framework, a higher education institution is directed to appoint a standing advisory committee whose charge is to oversee both the strategic plan for emergency management and the formal operational safety plan. The advisory committee, in consultation with internal and external stakeholders, will discuss the Standards as well as other factors that will impact on the operational safety plan goals, such as identities of elected officials and election timelines, the higher education institution's command staff, and projections for the financial budget (EMAP, 2019). Furthermore, this advisory committee would also schedule monthly and annual meetings, personnel training, and other activities that contribute to the overall future enhancement of emergency management operations (EMAP, 2019; ISU, 2019; ISU, 2020). For example, at the study's blue light institution, the ISU emergency management team (advisory committee) developed a resource gap analysis management tool, which inventoried available resources, identified known shortfalls, and then placed this information in a standalone document that then informed the institution's operational safety plan (EMAP, 2019; ISU, 2019; ISU, 2018a). In analyzing both documents and the interview from ISU (2019; 2020) representative, it was apparent that the EMAP Standards offer a comprehensive set of benchmarks that an institution's emergency management team could readily incorporate into their operational safety plan design and implementation. Therefore, results from this study strongly support the recommendation that colleges, universities, and their affiliates obtain formal EMAP accreditation; the principles set forth in the Standards provide invaluable returns on investment that any institution would benefit from in terms of protecting life, limb, and property.

THEORETICAL IMPLICATIONS

When the document analysis protocol was originally conceived, it organized disparate lines of research into a framework that could be applied to the qualitative coding of operational safety plan documents and interviews. While the extant literature could plausibly be categorized into the six resultant themes utilized for this study, the overall field is characterized by individual research teams that focus on specific aspects of operational safety planning, yet this area of inquiry is not dominated by any one theoretical construct that definitively delineates "best practices" for design and implementation of these documents (Asmussen & Creswell, 2013; Bauman, 2017; Blair & Martaindale, 2013; Dahl, Bonham, & Reddington, 2016; Inskeep, 2019; NCCPS, 2016b; Rasmussen, 2019; Thompson, Price, Mrdjenovich, & Khubchandani, 2009). In fact, the field continues to primarily focus on descriptive studies that use surveys to assess either stakeholders' perceptions of crimes and safety on campus or effectiveness of potential strategies for enhancing individuals' sense of safety (Ford & Frei, 2016; Hughes, White, & Hertz, 2008; Schafer, Heiple, Giblin, & Burruss, 2010; Sheldon, 2018; Thompson et al., 2009; Zugazaga, Werner, Clifford, Weaver, & Ware, 2016). In aligning data results from this study to the published literature, one implication to emerge was the need for additional research to clarify, confirm, and expand explanatory research that addresses the aforementioned shortfall in theoretical understandings of design and implementation "best practices" for operational safety planning. Therefore, one reason for recommending that institutions incorporate the EMAP (2019) Standards into design and implementation of their operational safety plans is because it ". . . fosters . . . accountability . . . by establishing credible standards applied in a peer reviewed Assessment and Accreditation Process" (p. 3).

Higher education institutions in Virginia are legally mandated to develop a plan for emergencies, one of several state and federal laws that dictates how colleges, universities, and their affiliates must prepare and respond to crisis incidents (Code of Virginia §23.1-804; Mumper, Gladieux, King, & Corrigan, 2016). Under EMAP's (2019) Standards and peer-reviewed accreditation process, qualified emergency managers, along with their teams and incident commanders (ICs), have the authority to design and implement an operational safety plan that is grounded in the most up-to-date ". . . American National Standard . . . [that] continues to evolve to represent the best in emergency management . . . and is revised on a three-year cycle . . ." (EMAP, 2019, p. 3). Under Open Systems Theory, each college, university, or their affiliates ". . . exists in a specific physical, technological, cultural, and social environment to which it must adapt" (Scott & Davis, 2007, p. 19). At the onset of this project, interactions between an organization (e.g., higher education institution) and its environment were conceptualized as ". . . a source of opportunities and constraints, demands and threats" (Scott & Davis, 2007, p. 20). This included acquisitions of necessary resources and coordination with local, state, and federal emergency management personnel (Dow & Cutter, 2000; Duryea, 1973; Scott & Davis, 2007; Sheldon, 2018; Weick, 1976). However, an additional theoretical implication from this study would be expansion of the original application of Open Systems Theory to include not only resource acquisition and external coordination for operational safety plans, but also incorporation of the external EMAP Standards resource that stipulates concurrent formulation of multi-year strategic plans for emergency management (EMAP, 2019; Lawrence & Lorsch, 1967; Orlikowski, 1992). Such short-term and long-term planning would expand understandings of operational safety plan design and implementation, which would enhance overall safety and mitigate liability for the institution (Blanchard & Baez, 2016; EMAP, 2019; Fox & Savage, 2009; Mumper et al., 2016; Randazzo & Cameron, 2012; Randazzo & Plummer, 2009).

At the onset on this study, Rational Choice Theory was utilized to demonstrate that criminal behavior (i.e., manmade disasters) could be understood through the lens of rationalization; that is, a crime is a result of rational thought-out behavior (Bouffard & Exum, 2013; Criminal Justice, 2019; Cornish & Clarke, 1986). Even though some may argue against rational motivation behind criminality, it is prudent to consider that irrational tendencies exist. While selection of Rational Choice Theory for understanding operational safety plans for manmade disasters remains valid, one final theoretical implication to emerge from data analysis was that application of this theory to the research questions should be expanded to include the premise that all people are rational and weigh their decisions based on perceived benefits (Bouffard & Exum, 2013; Cornish & Clarke, 1986; Grasmick & Bursik, 1990; Kubrin, Stucky, & Krohn, 2009). To clarify, it became evident during analysis of the interviews in particular that higher education emergency managers, their support teams, and senior administrators rationalized decisions regarding the design and implementation of their operational safety plans based on perceived costs and benefits (Bouffard & Exum, 2013; Criminal Justice, 2019; Cornish & Clarke, 1986; Dow & Cutter, 2000; Ford & Frei, 2016; Sheldon, 2018). To illustrate, the ODU (2020) representative, when asked why they were not EMAP accredited, stated

> . . . there is a financial component to that too. It ain't cheap to become accredited because you have to pay for an all-inclusive visit by a team to come here so it's between $5,000 to $10,000 dollars, which normally isn't bad, but right now given what we're dealing with [referring to COVID-19] and anticipating 15 percent budget cuts across the board it's going to be harder to swallow . . . (ODU, 2020)

The Virginia interview representatives all mentioned financial constraints, which impacted prioritization of various design and implementation factors in their operational safety plans. However, at ISU, one perk of having budgeted the time and resources toward obtaining an EMAP certification was assistance with locating and applying for additional grant funds that cover resource procurement and allocation; that is, EMAP certification supports the HOW an institution receives, manages, and applies for funds toward its operational safety plan (EMAP, 2019). Additional benefits to EMAP (2019)-certified colleges, universities, and their affiliates include scalable, standards-based procedures that are reasonable to comply with regarding WHO is responsible for the operational safety plan process and multi-year strategic planning, WHEN they will do it, and WHAT the specifications (i.e., administration and financial functions) are. In addition, EMAP institutions, like ISU, create detailed documents that address additional steps to take during a disaster that clearly identifies pertinent personnel, their responsibilities, and leadership succession (e.g., Continuity of Operations Plan, Hazard Mitigation Plan, Continuity of Government Plan, etc.). Utilization of the resources and certification process provided by EMAP affords higher education institutions and their affiliates the opportunity to firmly ground their emergency management operations (i.e., operational safely and multi-year strategic planning) in peer-reviewed guidelines that are periodically updated by the EMAP Commission to reflect the best known practices for keeping a campus community safe from natural and manmade disasters (EMAP, 2019). In re-evaluating the cost-benefit equation to take into consideration the extensive benefits of expanding beyond what is simply offered by NIMS and ICS, an institution's emergency management personnel should make the rational choice in favor of obtaining an EMAP accreditation for their institution's operational safety plans.

Epilogue

Applications Beyond the College Quadrangle

Throughout this book, great care has been taken to document the status of crisis preparedness at college-affiliated institutions. In doing so, the central role of a well-designed operational safety plan in mitigating and reducing the impacts of natural and manmade crises on these organizations has been argued for. The primary source of this book's findings is from public community colleges, universities, and graduate-affiliated research facilities. However, with over 4,400 higher education institutions in the United States alone, this book is intended more as a starting point for a continuing conversation about the importance of identifying the most salient guiding principles, implementation factors, and recommended "best practices" for the design and implementation of operational safety plans. By including perspectives from private institutions, for-profit colleges, and universities outside of the Commonwealth of Virginia (in states that do not necessarily mandate formal operational safety plans under their state codes), the overall picture of what constitutes the most effective practices for creating these plans would become richer and more complete.

However, crises are not confined to higher education institutions alone. Crises do not discriminate and it is unknown when or where the next tragedy will take place or who it will affect. For example, Hurricane Katrina not only disrupted the operations of Tulane University, Xavier University, and other colleges in the New Orleans area, but the storm surge, waters, and wind also destroyed businesses, neighborhoods, and critical infrastructures. In chapter 1, Open Systems Theory was used to illustrate how organizations (i.e., collectivities) are both responsive to and influenced by their environments. The rationale for utilizing Open Systems Theory in this book has been the recognition that college-affiliated operational safety plans are sensitive to both internal and external dynamics, and these factors intimately influence design and implementation decisions. Since Open Systems Theory can be utilized to understand other organizational types, the proposition to be examined in this concluding chapter is that the guiding principles, implementation factors, and recommended "best practices" (e.g., EMAP certification) advocated in this book are also broadly applicable to the multi-year strategic plans for crisis management at K–12 schools, businesses, churches, law enforcement, and state and local government agencies.

Throughout 2020 and 2021, the world has faced a devastating pandemic caused by the SARS-CoV-2 virus (COVID-19). Even though COVID-19 was not the first (nor will it be the last) pandemic that America will face, it has been, however, one of the most stressful experiences that anyone could endure. One of the primary factors contributing to the ensuing chaos has been a lack of preparation for a pandemic, as illustrated by the fact that four out of the five operational safety plans examined for this book did not even have a section for planning and responding to a biological event (only Eastern Virginia Medical School [EVMS] addressed this contingency). With the lack of adequate knowledge, education, and leadership, many citizens were left to rely on information available on the internet and social media to inform their personal responses.

Even now, more than a year and a half later, knowledge about exactly how the original virus outbreak in Wuhan, China, unfolded still remains spotty at best. The leading hypothesis is that an infected animal passed through the Huanan wet market, and the virus jumped the species barrier when a human came in contact with that animal. What is known is that cases of a mysterious respiratory illness, later identified as COVID-19, was spiking as of December 2019, but given basic virology dynamics, the SARS-CoV-2 virus probably was in circulation around Wuhan perhaps as early as October or November of 2019. Concurrently, China was reassuring the rest of the world that it had this situation under control, most notably through a complete lockdown of the province in which Wuhan is located: no one was allowed in and no one was allowed out. As a result, few people outside of China recognized the potential for this mystery illness to become a major crisis.

To illustrate: in the United States, the Trump administration and Democrats in Congress were embroiled in the President's first impeachment trial over his call to the Ukrainian President, Volodymyr Zelenskyy, earlier that summer. In a series of recorded interviews with Washington Post associate editor, Bob Woodward, President Trump admitted that he understood the severity of the growing COVID-19 pandemic as early as February 2020 ("more deadly than even your strenuous flu") (Gittleson, 2020, p. 1). Furthermore, he told Mr. Woodward that he deliberately downplayed the seriousness of what was happening so as not to ". . . create a panic" (Gittleson, 2020, p. 1) and even complimented Chinese President Xi Jinping for his government's efforts to contain the virus. Despite President Trump's public reassurances, he was told as early as January 28, 2020, that ". . . the virus would be the biggest national security threat of his presidency" (Gittleson, 2020, p. 1; Woodward, 2020). Thus, behind the scenes, the Trump administration, the Centers for Disease Control, and the National Institutes of Health (including Dr. Anthony Fauci) discussed possible contingencies, should the virus appear in the United States, but there was a disconnect between leadership choices and proposed safety precautions.

Down Pennsylvania Avenue, Congressional Democrats in the House of Representatives were holding hearings and drafting articles of impeachment against Trump. In between Democratic sparring with Trump officials over subpoenas to testify and then their attempts to persuade their Republican colleagues of the appropriateness of impeaching the President for his attempted "quid pro quo" (Committee on the Judiciary, 116th United States Congress, 2019), the Senate Health and Foreign Relations Committees held an intelligence briefing at the end of January 2020 for all Senators regarding the novel coronavirus and developments in China. By March 2020, Senators were sharing their weekly intelligence updates with their counterparts in the House of Representatives. How widely that information was known across the entire Congressional body though is unclear, but it was not deemed urgent enough to break into the dominant conversation of the day: should Congress impeach the President? While it is open to debate how much attention Congress might have paid to the situation in China had there been no impeachment proceedings, it is clear that the leadership choices of the Trump White House and Congressional Republicans in downplaying the situation's seriousness contributed to an under-prepared health sector and general public.

Interestingly, back in late 2016 and early 2017, officials from the outgoing Obama administration met with their incoming Trump counterparts in order to brief them on their respective roles, which traditionally ensure an uninterrupted, smooth presidential transition. Several of the lesser-known meetings involved tabletop exercises during which officials planned for a pandemic-like situation using guidelines set forth in a "pandemic playbook" (Knight, 2020, p. 1). This document was a nearly seventy-page guidebook developed in 2016 by the National Security Council (similar versions were created by the U.S. Department of Health & Human Services and the Centers for Disease Control & Prevention) incorporating lessons learned from the Ebola and Zika virus outbreaks (Knight, 2020). In addition to providing guidance for executing a coordinated federal government response, the "pandemic playbook" (Knight, 2020, p. 1) specifically identified various infectious disease threats (including novel coronaviruses) that were cause for concern. This document also collected not only the Obama administration's additional experience with the 2009 H1N1 outbreak, but also lessons learned from responses developed during the George W. Bush's administration to the SARS-1, MERS, and avian flu outbreaks in Asia (Paules, Eisinger, Marston, & Fauci, 2017; Obama, 2020). For the outbreaks that occurred in both the Bush and Obama administrations, they were limited in their impacts on everyday life in the United States because both Presidents made leadership choices based on information provided to them by experts (e.g., medical professionals, intelligence analysts, etc.).

On top of the pandemic's ongoing devastation, on April 29, 2021, a suspected Russian-linked cyber-hacking gang (REvil) launched a ransomware attack on a pipeline infrastructure system owned by the American oil company, Colonial Pipeline, located in Houston, TX (Turton & Mehrotra, 2021). By targeting one of the primary pipelines that supplies gasoline and jet fuel to the Southeastern region of the United States, the cyber attack effectively interrupted operations of the computerized equipment that maintains and manages this fuel pipeline (Turton & Jacobs, 2021). After preventing Colonial Pipeline's employees access to their own accounts and systems, the hackers demanded a ransom of 4.4 million dollars, which the company paid (Shaban, Naskashima, and Lerman, 2021). This technological crisis was further compounded by state governors who declared states of emergency, panicking their residents and creating local fuel shortages as individuals stockpiled gasoline (including in non-sanctioned plastic bags). Even though overall there was plenty of fuel available (distribution was just temporarily disrupted), the whole scenario highlighted a growing potential for extreme calamity caused by a technological crisis born out of our ever-increasing integration of technology with our global supply chains and human irrationality.

Having succeeded in extorting money from Colonial Pipeline, the exact same Russian ransomware gang struck less than a month later, this time hitting the multinational meat packing firm JBS (Shaban, Naskashima, & Lerman, 2021). As this nation's largest beef processor and major supplier of poultry and pork, JBS had to suspend operations temporarily when technology personnel noticed irregularities in their servers' functioning as well as a ransom note (Bunge, 2021). Had the company not paid the $11 million ransom, the forced shutdown almost certainly would have threatened the U.S. food chain at a sensitive time when the nation was attempting to emerge from the COVID-19 pandemic. Furthermore, a lengthy shutdown would have accelerated rises in meat pricing at the height of the summer cookout season (Bunge, 2021; Shaban et al., 2021). Designing and implementing operational safety plans for protecting essential-service providers' (e.g., hospitals, transport operators, food processing plants, etc.) information technology (IT) infrastructure became even more urgent after REvil's third wave of ransonware attacks struck several managed-service providers, companies that provide IT services to thousands of businesses worldwide. Despite President Biden's strongly worded warning to Russian President Vladmir Putin as well as an executive order that sets new standards of security for federal networks, there is only so much that law enforcement and the government are able to do when perpetrators are beyond U.S. jurisdiction (Turton & Jacobs, 2021; The White House, 2021). In spite of these limitations, organizations are not completely helpless when it comes to operational safety planning for technological (and other) crises if company leadership are proactive in adopting operational safety plans that contain effective strategies for preventing or mitigating impacts of an untimely cyber attack (Ordonez, 2021).

One of the more striking trends to emerge from the case studies done for this book was the importance that emergency managers attached to resource availability, especially financial resources, in justifying their decisions regarding what (or what not) to include when designing their operational safety plans. Regardless of whether a threat might come from increased gun access by mentally disturbed individuals, natural disasters, biological events, or technological crises, most emergency managers explained that their budgets were constrained, that they could not do everything that they might otherwise want to do because administrators did not necessarily prioritize funding for operational safety planning and preparedness. Only Idaho State University adopted the mantra that "whatever is needed will be provided, regardless of cost, when it comes to campus community safety." Many agencies, departments, businesses, etc. have a vision or mission statement that outlines their organizations' core values and beliefs. However, there can be substantial disparities between those statements (the ideal) and organizational actions (the reality). If one wishes to understand what an organization truly values, then it might be illuminating to take an audit (or accounting) of what their budget allocates money for. As one frustrated emergency responder pointed out, "how does one place a price on human safety?" The answer is that great leaders recognize that one cannot place a price on human safety and organizational security; the difference between Idaho State University and the leadership of the frustrated emergency responder lay in contrasting leadership philosophies that factored operational safety planning differently when calculating a path to organizational success. It will be argued that operational safety planners are better off in terms of success if they utilize a proactive approach that incorporates the guiding principles, implementation factors and "best practices" recommended here.

LEADERSHIP PHILOSOPHY

Over a career based on training, experience, and observation, a few corner-stones of leadership have become readily apparent: being proactive, motivated, and driven. These are further elaborated on the author's philosophy:

> As an Operational Safety Planner, I take the oath of to be honest, trustworthy, and demonstrate integrity (i.e., putting people first). I shall respectfully honor all people and seek their input as I strive to safeguard their livelihoods and endeavors at our organization. As for my team, I shall teach them, through education and experience, the importance of motivation, dedication, commitment, and safety in designing and implementing an effective operational safety plan. I shall encourage them that hard work, sacrifice, and having a vision thereof, not only brings respect to them but creates opportunities to advance in their careers and leadership potential. My goal as their leader is to instill principles such as veracity, teamwork, and to nurture a habit of lifelong learning through training to achieve top results. I am reminded that knowledge is power and Harry S. Truman said it best, "Not all Readers are Leaders, but all Leaders are Readers." I shall encourage open communication with all stakeholders to stimulate innovative ideas so as to create an atmosphere that is both challenging and enthusiastic. I shall strive to inspire my supervisors to continually keep an open mind, be proactive, and help them to recognize the positive impact they have on others through their leadership example. As Frank Gaines said, "Only he who can see the invisible can do the impossible." John Maxwell, "A leader is one who knows the way, goes the way, and shows the way." And Dwight Eisenhower, "Leadership is the art of getting someone else to do something you want done because he wants to do it."

In studying leadership and great leaders, journaling is an important task for jotting down ideas, inspiration, and reflections. Many leaders have acknowledged the essential nature of journaling to sorting out their thoughts and then subsequently executing these ideas in partnership with others to meet objectives. For example, I (like other leaders) keep a note pad by my bedside because useful ideas tend to manifest themselves in the middle of the night. More often than not, I will spring out of bed and scribble notes down in the dark so as to not forget them by the morning light. Even if I do not use those notes immediately, I have found that having a record and looking back over it after some passage of time can provide novel applications of those thoughts that were not readily apparent at the time I wrote them down. What follows are some examples of this very phenomenon recreated from my notes for this book.

> How did journaling help me in understanding the relationship between operational safety planning and leadership styles?

First and foremost, I must say that I found that journaling to be quite interesting because I did not anticipate going back to read and reflect on my previous work, which was intended to capture feelings and thoughts in a short amount of time (at that previous point in time). After reading and re-reading my journal entries, I did not quite recognize myself in my own writings. For example, I wrote quite a bit about this idea that life is either "this or that," "black or white [no gray area]," "good or bad," or "right or wrong." This mentality originated with the training I received in a police academy that I attended at age twenty-two. Members of the training academy made us feel that it was us (cops) against them (the public), which is where the "T" Truth mentality was born. So toward the beginning of my journal reflection, one question that needed to be asked was how the concept(s) made me think differently. I found that my persistent capital "T" Truth is not so capital anymore. I found that I have some lowercase "t" truth in myself, which is not so bad after all. I learned from this that everyone has a very unique walk in life and what they value should be given the same consideration, regardless of who they are and what they believe. In fact, I used a famous film, *Short Circuit*, as an analogy to illustrate that things are not "always as they seem." In the movie *Number 5* (also known as *Johnny Five*) gave a computer-generated analysis of the tomato soup that was poured onto a piece of paper by the NOVA employee. When the robot first responded, he sounded like me (i.e., having that "T" Truth mindset), but when he took a closer look, he said that (referring to the symbol that the soup made when it was poured onto the paper) it resembled a butterfly, a maple leaf, etc. (i.e., "t" truth). How the robot spoke is how I feel right now.

What struck me as I reread this set of journal entries was how it has informed my perception of operational safety planning and the importance of leadership. When I started this research, I had a very capital "T" Truth approach to operational safety planning; that is, I was wholly focused on "keeping people safe" without regard to context or organizational dynamics. The mere habit of writing my thoughts down was indicative of my proactive approach to all things in my professional career. Furthermore, the singular focus on "keeping people safe" is an artifact of my law enforcement training; for sixteen plus years, my job has been to keep people safe. Given the amount of time between when I originally made this journal entry and now, I most certainly did not remember these thoughts until I went back and re-read the entries for a different purpose. However, I am thankful that I did because it has helped to crystallize my leadership philosophy for this chapter. In sharing this episode with you, it demonstrates the importance of keeping an open mind and having the ability to be flexible in application of ideas. Because I went back, I was reminded of my transition from viewing operational safety planning as a capital "T" Truth (keeping people safe) exercise to a lowercase "t" truth one (how to keep people safe). There were key differences between what I found in the operational safety plans of non-EMAP certified institutions and Idaho State University (an EMAP-certified institution), which result in large part from leadership choices that are more reactive versus proactive.

> What other insights regarding operational safety planning and leadership came to me as I re-read my journal entries?

What surprised me most about the journal reflecting was that things are not always as they seem and that it is imperative that we all look at situations with our biases and other peoples' biases side by side (coexistence if you will). In fact, my series of journals' entries reminds me of the training that I had in the academy about investigating domestic violence. In that training, we were instructed to look at both sides, put our biases to the side, and apply the law as necessary (in that if we can determine the initial aggressor, make an arrest). Even though the law was followed, a judge (nine times out ten) will dismiss a domestic violence charge because the parties kissed and madeup. The ironic piece is that this dichotomy of listening to both sides and remaining unbiased is not what law enforcement supervision follows when dealing with their own personnel. However, I feel that people should listen and apply Phil Collins's song titled "Both Sides of the Story" when dealing with all issues in life, which describes multiple points of view of a situation side by side (coexistence). In fact, part of the lyrics are as follows:

> We always need to hear both sides of the story
> And the lights are all on, the world is watching now
> people looking for truth, we must not fail them now
> be sure, before we close our eyes
> don't walk away from here
> 'til you hear both sides

In the song's video, there was a picture depicting police officers in which the author was suggesting that they, too, should listen to both sides of the story (after all, it is their job). The moral of the story here is to stop and listen to others and appreciate someone else's lifestyle while self-reflecting on your own life and not judge others. We will never be able to fully understand someone's life, but what we can do is to treat others as we would like to be treated, Capital "T" Truth in a new light.

In emphasizing the importance of lowercase "t" truth to leadership choices regarding the design and implementation of operational safety plans (how to keep people safe), I wish to also draw the readers' attention to the contributions

Figure E.1.
Picture sketched by author, Antonio Passaro, Jr.

their stakeholders (the people they are keeping safe) can make to their organizational plans' success. While all institutions examined in this book solicited intermittent feedback from their campus communities for operational safety planning, only Idaho State University (an EMAP-certified organization) makes this an ongoing and integral part of their emergency management operations. Additionally, although the research presented in this work was done through my law enforcement lens, I intentionally juxtapose my professional recollections of the Virginia Tech massacre in the prologue with that of Dr. Weiss's memories as a student experiencing an active shooter incident at Penn State in her foreword. Both perspectives are important in advancing the conversation about what guiding principles, implementation factors and recommended "best practices" would enhance the effectiveness of operational safety plans.

How has this research contributed to my learning and growth as a leader and as an operational safety planner?

In answering this question, I reference figure E.2. The person looking in the binoculars should not only be looking at things in front of him (or her), but also things that are beyond his (or her) reach. Sometimes we only see things as we want to see them based on our own walk of life, but if we were to look beyond what is there, we might find reasons for making different leadership choices that are more inclusive of other people's perspectives (i.e., understand what our stakeholders need to feel safe); the same way we would like others to take into consideration our needs during a crisis.

Figure E.2.
Picture sketched by author, Antonio Passaro, Jr.

CONCLUSION

Although the concept of operational safety plans for natural, manmade, biological, and technological disasters has been practically implemented for decades by local, state, and federal agencies, its legal application at higher education institutions has only occurred formally in the wake of the Virginia Tech
massacre in 2007. Research over the past fourteen years has been focused
on perceptions of safety and preparedness or enhancing specific aspects of
an emergency response for future incidents (i.e., improved communication).
While the federal government has developed the NIMS and ICS resources to
guide design and implementation of operational safety plans, colleges, universities, and their affiliates remain largely uninformed about other available
resources that can significantly enhance their emergency management operations in the short- and long-term. Guidelines such as the EMAP Standards,
which are backed by the American National Standards Institute (ANSI), provide institutions with peer-reviewed information regarding effective operational safety and multi-year strategic planning for emergency management.
Along with the NCCPS, REMS TA, and DRU listserv, among others, these
resources offer critical insights for practical use as well as starting points
for research inquiries that further advance theoretical understandings of the
necessary guiding principles, implementation factors and "best practices" for

operational safety planning. It goes without saying that organizational leaders should have a proactive approach when it comes to "safety;" that is, preparing for the unexpected. It is not "if," it is "when" will the next major event hit; it IS coming. Adoption of the EMAP Standards and additional resources mentioned in this book not only streamline and enhance the operational safety plan process in compliance with various legal mandates, but it also brings more organizations closer to the ideal enshrined in Cicero's axiom, "Salus populi suprema lex (the safety of the people is the highest law)."

Appendix A

Operational Safety Plan Analysis Protocol

There are a number of articles that address particular aspects of design and implementation of operational safety plans (Ford & Frei, 2016; Virginia Tech Review Panel, 2007). Some major themes found in this literature are emergency communication protocols, training of first responders and campus stakeholders (i.e., faculty, staff, and students), and resource procurement and allocation (Blair & Martaindale, 2013; Briggs & Kennedy, 2016; Sheldon, 2018). Moreover, the vast majority of research in this area examines the issue primarily from the perspective of manmade disasters (e.g., active shooter situation, violent crime, assault, etc.) (Becker, 2004; Fox & Savage, 2009; Sheldon, 2018; Traynor, 2018). While a great deal of attention has been placed on developing effective strategies for responding to crisis, a number of studies also pointed out important limitations that were considered when proposing the "best practices" for design and implementation of operational safety plans for both natural and manmade disasters made in this book (Fox & Savage, 2009; Traynor, 2012).

The creation of a document analysis protocol for this qualitative research was to facilitate the author's collection, sorting, and analysis of data from college-affiliated institutional operational safety plans. This protocol helped to ground this book's findings in the field's literature. Thus, when the author recommended guiding principles, critical factors, and "best practices" for the design and implementation of operational safety plans, they resulted from design-based research that acknowledged the following most common themes found in the literature: *Training, Resources, Communication, Emergency Threat, Coordination, and Emergency Management* (Dede, Ketelhut, Whitehouse, Breit, & McCloskey, 2009).

TRAINING

The next theme of interest is Training whereby organizations train their campus community in preparation for the possibility of a natural or manmade crisis. There could be potentially two components to this training (NCCPS, 2016b; NDPC, 2018). First, it would be important to train and educate faculty and staff regarding how they should respond to manmade and natural disaster situations using lectures, mock scenarios, training videos, etc. Furthermore, students could be offered similar types of training that are geared toward their positions as students. Second, first responders are given advanced training on how to keep people safe during a natural or manmade emergency (Cooper & Block, 2006; NCCPS, 2016b; NDPC, 2018). Training is an essential component in the design and implementation of a successful operational safety plan because the better equipped the college community is, the higher probability of its survival (Cowen & Seifter, 2018; Harrison, 2014).

Blair and Martaindale's (2013) study focused on active shooter events from 2000 to 2010 and showed that training was essential for both indoor and outdoor events. In fact, their study revealed of the 84 active shooter events, most attacks occurred at businesses (37%), schools (34%), or outdoor public places (17%). The most common weapons used by the perpetrator were a pistol (60%), rifle (27%), and shotgun (10%), and that 49% of the attacks ended before the police arrived on scene (Blair & Martaindale, 2013). Therefore, designers of operational safety plans can take these statistics into account when tailoring advanced training for first responders that prepare them accordingly, especially in the area of outdoors attacks, lifesaving first aid that stabilizes victims while securing a location, and training/equipping units with patrol rifles and hard body armor that can withstand weaponry used by an active shooter (Blair & Martaindale, 2013; Brinsfield & Mitchell, 2015; DHS, 2018).

Briggs and Kennedy (2016) posited that mass shootings are rare and when these events occur, "they unfold quickly" (p. 3521), which is why a need to train potential victims on the idea of "Run, Hide, Fight" (p. 3521) exists. The premise of this specialized training, according to Briggs and Kennedy (2016), is that if victims display resistance while awaiting for law enforcement arrival, it can decrease the number of potential casualties even though the personal risk is high for injuries. In order to help understand what increases the chances of potential victims surviving an armed encounter with an active shooter, the authors ran simulations (i.e., active shooter scenarios) in which different variables were introduced (e.g., a victim fighting a shooter, a victim running, etc.). The results showed that any distraction can decrease the number of casualties overall. Ford and Frei's (2016) rationale in their study revealed that institutions must motivate individuals to want to train in the first place. They used several different outlets (e.g., email, text messaging, etc.) to determine which type would be more motivating. Results showed that emails with fear-based frames encouraged more individuals to complete the training video than any other message medium (Ford & Frei, 2016). However, it should be noted that this research follows from an assumption that watching a five-minute video on "Run. Hide. Fight." adequately prepares people for handling active shooters (Ford & Frei, 2016).

Training and education can also provide deterrence. First, if a potential shooter is aware that people are now trained, this might force the shooter to reconsider (Blair & Martaindale; 2013; Blair, Nichols, Burns, & Curnutt, 2013; Blair & Schweit, 2014). Second, the training will help to guide potential victims on what to do in case of such an emergency (i.e., finding cover, mitigate and reduce casualties, etc.) (Briggs & Kennedy, 2016; Ford & Frei, 2016). Finally, education can also provide the means by which administrators and campus safety personnel can identify additional strategies that can prevent an individual from ever becoming an active shooter; that is, enhancing the capabilities of the threat assessment team or mental health services on campus that diffuse angry or mentally ill individuals before they decide that their only option is to shoot other people (Evans, Bira, Gastelum, Weiss, & Vanderford, 2018; Fox & Savage, 2009; Lannon, 2014; Randazzo & Plummer, 2009). However, it is evident in the literature that college-affiliated administrators and safety personnel may not be able to always account for all variables affecting the outcome of a crisis event when planning and executing their training and education efforts (Blair & Martaindale; 2013; Briggs & Kennedy, 2016; Ford & Frei, 2016).

In the protocol, the *Training* theme examined those portions of an institution's operational safety plan that related to the goals and objectives, simulations and mock scenarios, and education materials that ensure a college-affiliated community is ready to respond when an actual natural or manmade crisis occurs. According to EMAP (2019), training "includes the assessment, development and implementation of training for Program officials, emergency management response personnel and the public" (p. 14). Research demonstrated that training for emergency responders and campus stakeholders is a beneficial and proven means for reducing and mitigating risks (Blair & Martaindale, 2013; Blair et al., 2013; Briggs & Kennedy, 2016; NCCPS, 2016b; NDPC, 2018; Schafer, Heiple, Giblin, & Burruss, 2010).

RESOURCES

Another theme found in the literature is Resources, which are goods and services needed in the design and implementation of operational safety planning.

There are several components to the Resources theme. For example, Blair and Martaindale's (2013) research ascertained the most common attributes describing active shooter situations (i.e., what weapons were used, the percentage of victim attacks on the assailant, location, etc.) so that police chief administrators might know what resources are needed for their officers to be on the same or better level than the criminal. In Traynor's (2012) research, he found that cell phone infrastructures most likely would be unable to handle the mass volume of text alerts needed to be sent during a crisis. In fact, in his case study of the Virginia Tech massacre (i.e., communication efforts), he calculated that it would have taken (with the cellular infrastructure available to campus officials on April 16, 2007) approximately fifteen minutes to send one text message to fifteen thousand recipients; VA Tech to date has approximately 30,500 students. Therefore, additional resources would probably be necessary for notifying the campus community during an emergency situation on campus (Fox & Savage, 2009; Traynor, 2012).

Cooper and Block (2006), in their case study of Hurricane Katrina, examined many aspects of the federal and state governments' responses, including the resources needed and their actual allocation in August 2005. To illustrate, Cooper and Block (2006) reported that during a simulation of a fictitious Category 3 Hurricane Pam, officials projected that, "300 boats, 800 body bags, 400 flashlights, 150 paddles, and 12 spare bilge plugs for small craft" (p. 19) were needed. In addition, approximately 40,000 volunteers and staff would be needed as well as "1.53 million gallons of water and 5.5 million pounds of ice to the area each day" (p. 19). In the implementation of this operational safety plan, authorities were constrained by the resources that were available, and yet they still planned to operate to their fullest capacity within these limitations (Cooper & Blocker, 2006). Furthermore, FEMA authorities promised to supplement whatever additional supplies would be needed in the event of a hurricane making catastrophic landfall in New Orleans, but during Hurricane Katrina it quickly became clear that relying on the federal government for assistance was futile (Cooper & Block, 2006). For example, FEMA personnel assured that they could provide one hundred thousand beds and equipment for mobile communication centers and video teleconferencing, but never delivered. In fact, when it was time for them to actually perform, they could neither provide the basics such as flashlights nor the vast quantity of water and ice needed (Cooper & Block, 2006).

When considering the literature regarding resources necessary for successful design and implementation of operational safety plans, it should be noted that authors are focused more on specific elements (equipment, infrastructures, and supplies needed) rather than human behavior (Blair & Martaindale, 2013; Cooper & Block, 2006; Fox & Savage, 2009; Traynor, 2012). Humans can overestimate their abilities and be overconfident in their conclusions. For example, in criminal justice research, it has been demonstrated that eyewitness testimony is frequently faulty, resulting in false accusations, susceptibility to planting of misinformation, and "persistent false memory" (Loftus, 2019, p. 498) (Hyman, Wulff, & Thomas, 2018; Stahl, 2009). Additionally, in novel situations which humans have little to no experience with, they tend to behave as if their memories of a previous event, no matter how much time has elapsed since the traumatic event or degree of impact (direct vs. indirect), are sufficient guide to prepare for future crisis (Barron & Yechiam, 2009; Kornell & Bjork, 2009). In regards to future events like a Hurricane Katrina, a Virginia Tech, etc., administrators and campus safety personnel may make judgement errors when designing resource needs and distribution without even realizing it until catastrophe strikes, even to the point of bias toward over-preparing (Albiges, 2018; Barron & Yechiam, 2009; Haselton, Nettle, & Murray, 2015; Rodgers, 2018).

The *Resources* theme accounted for all necessary equipment needed for preparation, response, and recovery to natural and manmade disasters. This also included procurement of materials and logistics (e.g., grants, donations, etc.), their distribution, and collaborations with local, state, and federal agencies (EMAP, 2019). Resource management frequently uses gap analysis in order to identify "resource needs and shortfalls that are prioritized and addressed through a variety of initiatives" (EMAP, 2019, p. 12). Successful resource procurement and distribution frequently determines whether or not an institutional response to crisis succeeds or fails (Barron & Yechiam, 2009; Blair & Martaindale, 2013; Cooper & Block, 2006; FEMA, 2011b; Fox & Savage, 2009; GAO, 2018; Hughes, White, & Hertz, 2008; NCCPS, 2016b; Schafer et al., 2010; Traynor, 2012).

COMMUNICATION

One of the areas found in the literature was the use of communication efforts and protocols during emergency disasters. The literature shows how college-affiliated institutions invested in a wide range of emergency communication systems (i.e., mass notification) in an effort to notify their students, faculty, and staff in an event of an emergency in a reasonable amount of time (Becker, 2004; Fox & Savage, 2009; Reynolds & Seeger, 2005; Sheldon, 2018; Traynor, 2012). Sheldon (2018) tested students' perceptions of crisis severity by generating two mock crisis situations (i.e., active shooter and tornado warning) in which he alerted individuals through the means of emergency alerts via text messages and social media. Results showed that students are more likely to notify their friends and family of a tornado warning via text messaging; meanwhile, they were more likely to share information about an active shooter scenario by word-of-mouth (Sheldon, 2018). While social media outlets were not taken as seriously as text messaging and word-of-mouth conversation, Sheldon (2018) demonstrated that students still perceived college shootings as more dangerous than natural disasters (i.e., shooters could harm more people). A similar study, done by Ford and Frei (2016), examined participants' motivation to complete training on how to handle an active shooter situation when alerted by email, text messaging, or Tweeting. An additional variable of interest was message framing (fear-based vs. direct information). Findings revealed that emails with fear-based frames led more individuals to complete the training video; however, the fear-based messages alone were not responsible for increasing participants' overall perception of personal campus safety, but rather watching the training video did (Ford & Frei, 2016).

Regardless of administrators' and campus safety personnel's efforts to effectively communicate during an emergency, each communication system has their own unique limitations with regard to impacts and perceptions of the crisis (Becker, 2004; Fox & Savage, 2009; Sheldon, 2018). Becker (2004) found, for example, that the public might be scared, may not totally believe the information source or that administrators would be entirely forthcoming about the crisis, and would be confused by difficult-to-understand jargon. The literature also pointed out communication difficulties; in that, in order for any communication systems to work, the campus community must buy into the idea and make an effort to participate in the system (e.g., downloading an alert app, providing the institution with their cell phone number, social media networks, etc.) (Becker, 2004; Fox & Savage, 2009; Sheldon, 2018). According to Fox and Savage (2009), it is critical, when sending out a mass notification about an emergency, that the communication is timely, relevant, and credible to its recipients; otherwise, too many of these alerts or misinformation will cause people to not pay attention (i.e., the "cry wolf" effect) (p. 1470). As examples, Fox and Savage (2009) reported that an alert meant for one campus of St. Johns University actually went out to all three while in another situation, an alert went out to the University of Iowa community when the active shooter was actually "many miles away on the opposite side of town, posing very little threat to the campus" (p. 1470). Finally, Traynor (2012) calculated that cell phone towers may not be able to handle emergency alerts in bulk when sent out at a given time. Using the September 11 terrorist attacks and the 2007 Virginia Tech shooting, it was determined that the sheer number of text messages needed to alert the respective populations would have overloaded the circuits and resulted in a situation not unlike "Denial of

Service (DoS) on the internet" (p. 993) in which text alerts would never be received by the intended parties.

This theme accounted for analysis of *Communication* protocols within college-affiliated operational safety plans. According to EMAP (2019), higher education administrators and campus safety personnel should have "communications, alert and notification, and warning plans that provide for using, maintaining, and augmenting the equipment necessary for efficient preparation for, response to and recovery from emergencies/disasters" (p. 13) (Becker, 2004; DHS, 2014; FEMA, 2011a; Ford & Frei, 2016; Fox & Savage, 2009; NCCPS, 2019; Sheldon, 2018; Traynor, 2012). Furthermore, communication before, during, and after a crisis can have a great deal of influence on perception of campus safety (Asmussen & Creswell, 2013; Dahl, Bonham, & Reddington, 2016; Reynolds & Seeger, 2005; Jennings, Gover, & Pudrzynska, 2007; Kaminski et al., 2010; Patton & Gregory, 2014; Shafer et al., 2010; Virginia Tech Review Panel, 2007; Zugazaga, Werner, Clifford, Weaver, & Ware, 2016).

EMERGENCY THREAT MANAGEMENT

Last but not least, the Enhancement theme accounts for procedure enhancement in the design and implementation of operational safety planning. Fox and Savage's (2009) research critically examined the seven most frequent recommendations made by university taskforces, the goal being to enhance their application for design and implementation of operational safety plans addressing active shooter scenarios on campus. To illustrate, the authors recommended that campus safety personnel should practice and train with scenarios, which can be an effective way to determine what works as well as to upgrade or enhance what is not working for emergency preparedness (Briggs & Kennedy, 2016; Fox & Savage, 2009; Ford & Frei, 2016; Sheldon, 2018; Stafford, 2014). Many higher education institutions do not have an emergency operational safety plan, and those who have "have not opened them in years. It is simply a notebook on the shelf that allows them to say that they have a 'plan' if there is an emergency on campus" (Stafford, 2014, p. 51). In fact, the U.S. Government Accountability Office (GAO) found that many higher education personnel are not aware of federal resources available to them for responding to a natural or manmade disaster, and recommended that federal agencies do a better job of providing this information to emergency planners at college-affiliated institutions (GAO, 2018). In reviewing major incidents that have occurred at other colleges or universities, institutional leadership can create or enhance an operational safety plan that is conducive to their campus environment and ". . . not just 'good in theory' but that . . . work in practice" (Stafford, 2014, p. 52) (Cooper & Block, 2014; Fox & Savage, 2009; Nelson, 2014; NCCPS, 2016b).

Recovery from a major incident may take months, if not years, to occur. For example, the 2011 EF-4 tornado that destroyed residential areas around the University of Alabama-Tuscaloosa left large numbers of faculty and students homeless. At the University of Alabama-Tuscaloosa, even three years later, faculty, staff, and students were still experiencing flashbacks to the event while the surrounding area still showed major signs of the storm's destruction (Nelson, 2014). In addition, the University of Iowa community began dealing with the Great Flood of 2008 in June (one of the top ten worst disasters in U.S. history), which would eventually destroy two million square feet of university facilities (Mason, 2014). Six years later, Mason (2014) shared that the recovery process still continued, including the reconstructing of three academic buildings that were to be completed in 2016. In the aftermath of such catastrophes, institutional leadership may find it advantageous to take this time to review, analyze, and enhance their policies for emergency operations. According to FEMA (2015), a post-disaster framework for these inquiries should include the following key components: 1) having a recovery coordination process, 2) assessing and evaluating the issues, 3) identifying key resources, and 4) encouraging resilience. In making such assessments, university officials, such as Mason (2014) and Nelson (2014), streamlined their operational safety plans, thereby maximizing their resources and enhancing future responses. To illustrate, Mason (2014) wrote "no one here had been trained for the specific tasks of long-term flood mitigation, but we are now" (p. 68). Highlighting the critical role leadership plays in coordinating both response and enhancement processes, Mason (2014) observed, ". . . that has happened because I had the wisdom, and some good fortune, to find the best people, coordinate and decide when needed, but mostly to get out of the way and let talented people do their jobs" (Mason, 2014, p. 73).

The final theme in this proposed document analysis protocol accounted for enhancing the design and implementation of operational safety plans after a crisis has occurred. "An Accredited Emergency Management Program has operational plans and procedures that are developed, coordinated and implemented among all stakeholders . . . [*Emergency Management*] describe emergency response, continuity of operations, continuity of government, and recovery from [all] emergencies/disasters" (EMAP, 2019, p. 9). A key to success in enhancing an institution's operational safety plans, given changing external and environmental realities, is being able to incorporate lessons learned from previous crises (Asmussen & Creswell, 2013; Blair & Martaindale, 2013; Cooper & Block, 2006; FEMA, 2015; Fox & Savage, 2009; Kaminski et al., 2010; Mason, 2014; NCCPS, 2016a; NCCPS, 2016b; Nelson, 2014; Shafer et al., 2010; Sheldon, 2018; Stafford, 2014; Thompson et al., 2009; Traynor, 2012; Virginia Tech Review Panel, 2007).

COORDINATION

Coordinating with federal, state, and local agency experts will allow administrators and safety personnel at higher education institutions to receive services in emergency preparation, response, and recovery. These service agencies include, but are not limited to, local, state, and federal police agencies, U.S. National Guard, FEMA, DHS, and the U.S. Departments of Justice (DOJ) and Education. These agencies can provide assistance with training, equipment, resources, and technical assistance (GAO, 2018).

An example of coordination between college-affiliated institutions and a government agency is the 1033 program designed to transfer military surplus (i.e., equipment and supplies) from the U.S. Department of Defense (DOD) to local, state, and campus law enforcement agencies throughout the nation. One major benefit to higher education institutions would be that a collaborative program such as the 1033 program allows personnel to purchase necessary equipment at lower cost, which can be a welcome efficiency in an era of shrinking budget support from state and federal sources (Bauman, 2017). The 1033 program stipulates that college or university officials only have to pay for the cost of transferring the equipment to their locations (Bauman, 2017). Unfortunately, college-affiliated administrators must weigh these budget savings benefits with the potential drawbacks of utilizing such a program. One such drawback, according to legislative counsel for the American Civil Liberties Union (ACLU), is that militarizing campus law enforcement may infringe on students' First Amendment rights (i.e., free speech and assembly) (Bauman, 2017). Heavily armed personnel on campus may give the appearance of hostility and warp the trust between the campus community and the police (Bauman, 2017; Kappeler & Kraska, 2013; Kraska, 2007; Kraska & Kappeler, 1997; Loftus, 2019). Mummolo (2018) demonstrated through several methodologies that militarized police departments result in their over-deployment to minority communities, and erosion of reputation among the public, especially among African Americans. Despite these concerns, campus safety personnel and the leadership of the International Association of Campus Law Enforcement Administrators (IACLEA) endorse having this equipment (e.g., armored vehicles, M-16 rifles, tactical gear, etc.) because it provides departments an advantage in the event of an active shooter, terrorist, or other violent threats, if they should occur (Bauman, 2017; Loftus, 2019;

Mummolo, 2018). To lessen concerns and misrepresentation, college and university officials must demonstrate certain protocols that 1) do not hinder free speech or create a hostile environment on campus, 2) do change the appearance so items do not look like military equipment, and 3) do require institutional approval (i.e., governing boards) before purchasing (Bauman, 2017).

When Hurricane Katrina struck New Orleans in August 2005, the lack of coordination between federal, state, and local agencies as well as with higher education institutions had dire consequences for colleges and universities in the city. Infrastructures at Dillard University, Southern University at New Orleans, and Xavier University, three historically black colleges and universities (HBCUS), as well as Tulane University were severely damaged by storm flooding and contamination, costing the respective institutions somewhere between $45 million and $650 million million to repair (Cowen & Seifter, 2018; Johnson & Rainey, 2007). Furthermore, enrolled students were transferred to other colleges and universities around the country for the remainder of the fall 2005 semester while faculty and staff were searching for employment elsewhere. All of these combined impacts ". . . threatened the very existence of [each] university . . ." (Cowen & Seifter, 2018, p. 6) as "large amounts of equipment and furniture, books and supplies, academic records and teaching materials were permanently damaged, first by winds, floods and poison-filled waters, next by post-hurricane fires, and finally by toxic mold and mildew (Johnson & Rainey, 2007, p. 102). Many of these consequences might have been averted had state and federal agencies properly maintained New Orleans' levee systems before a hurricane ever made landfall (Cooper & Block, 2006). Also, as part of the post-Katrina recovery, FEMA offered displaced students and their families the opportunity to apply for $2,000 in disaster assistance, but as with most other aspects of FEMA's response, there were challenges including students being asked to return relief funds because the agency decided that their dorms were not their permanent residents (Cooper & Block, 2006; Flack, 2017; Karlin, 2007; Johnson & Rainey, 2007). These after-effects resulted from the lack of coordination between government and higher education institutions, which are frequently underprepared to deal with crises of this magnitude on their own (Cowen & Seifter, 2018; Johnson & Rainey, 2007; Mason, 2014; Nelson, 2014).

The U.S. Government Accountability Office (GAO) personnel detailed how communication needs to improve between the federal emergency management resources and higher education institutions. GAO interviewed emergency management officials at eighteen colleges and then conducted document analysis and interviews with state government officials in Colorado, Kansas, and Virginia. Concurrently, they interviewed members from the Department of Homeland Security (DHS), Department of Justice (DOJ), and Department of Education about what resources they offer to colleges and universities for emergency preparedness. Results showed that all college emergency officials were aware of the National Incident Management System (NIMS). However, some of the institutional teams reported that they were unaware of additional governmental resources that are available to them, such as the 2013 Guide for Developing High-Quality Emergency Operations Plans, the NCCPS, or the Department of Education's Readiness and Emergency Management for Schools (REMS) Technical Assistance Center website (GAO, 2018). In order to enhance the activation and utilization of federally available resources for higher education emergency management, the GAO (2018) recommended that DHS, DOJ, and Education take additional steps to initiate contact with colleges and universities, and disseminate information about their resources (e.g., NCCPS, REMS, FBI's Campus Liaison Program, etc.) more effectively.

For this theme, the document analysis protocol searched for and examined sections related to *Coordination* when executing during a disaster. This included discussion of assistance from operating authorities, participation by stakeholders, and methods for debriefing (i.e., evaluating, maintaining, and revising operational safety plans) (EMAP, 2019). Of particular interest were protocols for multi-agency coordination and utilization of incident management systems, both of which were deemed essential "for clear and effective response and recovery" (EMAP, 2019, p. 11) (Asmussen & Creswell, 2013; Bauman, 2017; Copper & Block, 2006; Cowen & Seifter, 2018; FEMA, 2015; GAO, 2018; Hughes, White, & Hertz, 2008; Johnson & Rainey, 2007; Mason, 2014; Mumper et al., 2016; Nelson, 2014; Shafer et al., 2010; Thompson et al., 2009; Virginia Tech Review Panel, 2007).

EMERGENCY THREAT

In the wake of the Virginia Tech 2007 and Northern Illinois University 2008 mass shootings, state lawmakers enacted legal code sections that directed senior administrators and campus safety personnel to develop Care and Threat Assessment Teams in two states, Illinois and Virginia (Deisinger & Scalora, 2016; Randazzo & Plummer, 2007; Randazzo & Cameron, 2012). "CARE" team members help to match students in crisis with services offered by their institutions, especially when those individuals are unaware of the resources on campus. These programs are in place to provide students support from any trauma, health, or mental disabilities, whether or not they are registered under ADA or Section 504 (Eells & Rockland-Miller, 2011). If a student is brought to the attention of the CARE team and it is determined that the student may be a threat to themselves or others, his or her case will be referred to the

Threat Assessment Team (Hughes et al., 2008; Randazzo & Plummer, 2009). Randazzo & Cameron (2012) posited that:

> Threat assessment comprises four components: (a) learning of a person who may pose a threat; (b) gathering information about that person from multiple sources; (c) evaluating whether the person poses a threat of violence to others; and (d) developing and implementing an individualized plan to reduce any threat (this last component is often referred to as "threat management" or "case management). (p. 280)

For example, when evaluating a student that poses a threat on campus, it is imperative to consider the student's mental state and personal background (NCCPS, 2016b). Therefore, each individual is evaluated on a case-by-case basis so that a student is referred to the most appropriate support personnel (e.g., counseling, grievance, disability, and legal services) (Lannon, 2014; Randazzo & Cameron, 2012; Randazzo & Plummer, 2009; Virginia Tech Review Panel, 2007). It is important to note that effectiveness of this case management approach depends on these students not only being matched to suitable services, but also being monitored in an ongoing effort to alleviate the institution of any further risk, trauma, or threat (Randazzo & Plummer, 2009).

In creating the document analysis protocol, it was determined that operational safety plans needed to account for identifying what is a threat as well as how to mitigate, prevent, prepare, respond to, and recover. A college-affiliated institution's emergency management team "assesses the risk and vulnerability of people, property, the environment, and its own operations from [natural and manmade] hazards . . . [and] . . . identifies the natural and human-caused hazards that potentially impact the jurisdiction using multiple sources" (EMAP, 2019, p. 8). Previous studies had examined different aspects of threat assessment, including both natural (meteorology and climate change) and manmade (CARE and Threat Assessment Teams) events (Cooper & Block, 2006; FEMA, 2011a; IAEM, 2007; Inskeep, 2019; NCCPS, 2016a; NCCPS, 2016b; Oliver, 2009; Randazzo & Cameron, 2012; Rasmussen, 2019; Waugh, 2003; Zdiarski et al., 2007).

Appendix B

Methodology

The purpose of the multiple case study behind this book's findings was to compare the operational safety plans of a college, two universities, a research organization, and a graduate institution in the Commonwealth of Virginia and the state of Idaho. By doing so, this author sought to advance understanding of the most effective and salient strategies associated with operational safety plans as well as critical design and implementation factors. This research was guided by the following questions:

1. What principles guide the design of operational safety plans for college-affiliated institutions?
2. What factors found within college-affiliated educational institutions' operational safety plans are critical for successful implementation?
3. What are the "best practices" for operational safety plans that are utilized by college-affiliated institutions?

RESEARCH DESIGN

The primary means of data collection in the higher education operational safety planning field has been non-experimental, quantitative survey research in which participants responded to statements or questions utilizing Likert-type scales; then researchers analyzed the results using a variety of statistical methods (Kaminski, Koons-Witt, Thompson, & Weiss, 2010; Patton & Gregory, 2014; Thompson, Price, Mrdjenovich, & Khubchandani, 2009). Less often, researchers have employed qualitative or mixed methods research designs (Asmussen & Creswell, 2013; Patton & Gregory, 2014). Therefore, this project addressed a methodological gap in this research literature by identifying guiding principles, implementation factors, and candidate "best practices," potentially offering novel perspectives on the design and implementation of operational safety plans for college-affiliated institutions.

This qualitative research design used a comparative methodology utilizing multiple case studies (Berg, 2001; Creswell, 2013; Creswell & Plano Clark, 2011). First, the case study approach provides researchers with an opportunity to collect data that increase understanding of a general process, which extends beyond the boundaries of a particular project (Kaarbo & Beasley, 1999; Stake, 2000; Yin, 2018; Yin & Davis, 2007). In other words, Yin (2018) defined case study as "an empirical inquiry that: investigates a contemporary phenomenon (the "case") in depth and within its real-world context, especially when the boundaries between phenomenon and context may not be clearly evident" (p. 15). In addition, a comparative case study design allows for systematic exploratory and descriptive research comparing multiple bounded systems (i.e., "cases"); in this instance, a case is a unique operational safety plan (Kaarbo & Beasley, 1999; Yin & Davis, 2007). Results identified guiding principles (RQ1), implementation factors (RQ2), and candidate "best practices" (RQ3) recommended for development of future theories and enhancement of design-based research into operational safety plans for natural and manmade disasters. By utilizing this approach, the author was able to analyze cases for candidate "best practices" and then generalize overarching themes in order to develop a framework for future theory development and quantitative analysis.

SAMPLE

Purposeful sampling is a process that is mostly used in qualitative research to intentionally select "individuals, documents, situations, events, processes, times, and other aspects that can further develop . . . understanding and an explanation" (Krathwohl, 2004, pp. 259–260). The five institutions in this sample contributed to developing a comparative case study ". . . that will illustrate the range of settings or subjects [i.e., operational safety plan design and implementation]" (Bogdan & Biklen, 2007, p. 70; Creswell, 2013). In addition, one representative from each of the institutions was interviewed. (e.g., a director of safety operations who could offer additional insights into both political/legal and operational ramifications of their operational safety planning process). For those eight EMAP-certified institutions, an invitational letter to participate that requested access to their operational safety plan(s) and to identify them was sent to each university's safety director. Four of the eight EMAP institutions responded; three only offered their public version while the fourth offered their entire plan, which resulted them serving as the "blue light" institution here.

INSTRUMENTATION

The first instrument designed for this qualitative research was based on published literature, Standards from the Emergency Management Accreditation Program (EMAP), National Center for Campus Public Safety (NCCPS), International Association of Emergency Managers (IAEM), and International Association of Campus Law Enforcement Administrators (IACLEA). After examination of this literature, no template or outline for identifying operational safety plan "best practices" was found to exist, which could cover design principles and implementation factors related to natural and manmade disasters. Therefore, the document analysis protocol is found in appendix A.

In the document analysis protocol, there were six main themes for identifying candidate "best practices." The *Training* theme identified content in the operational safety plans that addresses the education and preparation of personnel so that they are ready to respond to an actual crisis (EMAP, 2019; NCCPS, 2016b; NDPC, 2018). *Resources* was a theme that identified whether or not an operational safety plan outlines the necessary equipment and manpower needed for the preparation, response to, and recovery from both natural and manmade disasters (EMAP, 2019; FEMA, 2011b; NCCPS, 2016a). The *Communication* theme examined the existence of protocols for interacting with stakeholders during a crisis in the institution's operational safety plans (DHS, 2014; EMAP, 2019; NLECTC, 2009). *Emergency Threat* theme identified the capabilities of an institution to recognize what constituted a "threat" and then how the management team would mitigate the effects of identified crises (DOJ, 2016; EMAP, 2019; NCCPS, 2016a). *Coordination* theme determined whether or not an operational safety plan contained information regarding coordination and execution during a crisis (EMAP, 2019; FEMA, 2012; FEMA, 2015). Finally, the *Emergency Management* theme determined what, if any, procedures are in an operational safety plan for initial design and then enhancement (i.e., lessons learned) of emergency management after a crisis (EMAP, 2019; FEMA, 2012; NCCPS, 2016b).

Second, for the interviews, the researcher created a protocol of several questions (appendix B) that allowed participants to explain the overall guiding principles, implementation factors, and what they perceived as "best practices" in their operational safety plans at their institutions. This protocol was developed using the information from the research literature, the research questions, and the methodological section of this chapter. The interview protocol was administered after the completion of the document analysis, for the purposes of follow-up and clarification.

DATA COLLECTION PROCEDURES

The researcher purposefully selected college-affiliated organizations within the Commonwealth of Virginia as data sources (Berg, 2001; Creswell, 2013). Three were higher education institutions, one was a joint graduate school and research facility, and one was a research center that participates in collaborative work partnerships with local universities; all had crisis and emergency management plans (i.e., their operational safety plans). The main emergency management point of contact was identified for each institution because operational safety plans were not necessarily publicly available on institutional websites. These individuals were contacted via email, phone or in-person and the premise of this research was explained, along with a request for access to the documents for review. Participants were also asked for consent to publicly identify them in this study's findings. Once approval was obtained, the operational safety plans were retrieved as electronic or hardcopy forms for subsequent analysis with no modifications to their original language. All documents were stored in a secure digital format to which only the researcher had access (O'Leary, 2014).

Once the document analysis was completed, the researcher then interviewed one representative (e.g., Director of Public Safety) from each of the selected institutions' emergency management team for approximately thirty minutes using the open-ended interview protocol. Prior to the start of each interview, the participant signed a confidentiality agreement that explained to them how their identities and responses would be protected from identification (appendix C). Interviews were then recorded using a digital recording device with the respondent's informed consent (appendix D), and later transcribed into a written record with names of interviewees redacted.

DATA ANALYSIS

The primary analytical techniques used in this research were comparative case study methodologies, such as document analysis and semi-structured interviews (Bowen, 2009; Stake, 2000; Yin, 2018). Document analysis consisted of collecting, assessing, and synthesizing informational data from each operational safety plan, which was later organized according to the themes outlined in the document analysis protocol (Bowen, 2009; Creswell, 2013). The operational safety plans were analyzed in the following order: the three higher education institutions, the joint graduate school/research facility, and the research center.

After transcription, the researcher read through each transcript and initially performed open, descriptive coding (Berg, 2001; Creswell, 2013; Maxwell,

2005). This process converted highlighted interview segments into tentative labels (code words) that captured the gist of what interviewees said. After the code words were produced from separate transcripts, data were pooled and analyzed in aggregate in order to determine their overall fit with the six themes and to assess the viability of the document analysis protocol as a framework for identifying guiding principles, implementation factors, and candidate "best practices."

As each plan was initially explored, details regarding layout, areas of emphasis, and potential threats were noted, along with any other information that shed light on the unique process by which that particular institution designed and implemented its operational safety plan (Bowen, 2009; O'Leary, 2014). This information was recorded in the form of a series of memos that also notated the researcher's personal biases (Creswell, 2013). Once all possible subjectivities were identified, the operational safety plan underwent a second, more detailed analysis of its content to identify such things as its style, purpose, intended audience, and relevant words and phrases regarding strategies and components necessary for effective operational safety plans (Altheide & Schneider, 2017; Bowen, 2009; O'Leary, 2014). In addition, through reading and re-reading each operational safety plan a second time, the document analysis protocol was applied to the plans' content such that data could be collected for each of the six themes (Altheide & Schneider, 2017; Bowen, 2009; O'Leary, 2014). For example, the college-affiliated institution's plan was scanned for any language related to "training." If a match was found, then it was coded as evidence in support of the Training theme; concurrently, language that related to any of the other five themes was similarly coded. The researcher tallied raw data for frequency of protocol theme occurrence and compared the results with those obtained from an independent reviewer before completing the document coding analysis. Interviews provided corroborating data regarding guiding principles, implementation factors, and "best practices." After transcription and initial coding analysis, the researcher consulted with informants to ensure accuracy. Final results were then presented using tables and charts, supplemented with representative quotes illustrating guiding principles, implementation factors, and candidate "best practices" associated with design and implementation of operational safety plans.

LIMITATIONS

This qualitative multiple case study of operational safety plans utilized institutions located primarily in the Commonwealth of Virginia. In addition, the four Virginia institutions were exclusively found within the Hampton Roads region. This precluded institutional perspectives from not only other geographical areas in Virginia, but also other parts of the country. While Idaho State University did provide some geographic diversity to the analysis, it still was only a single institution. Furthermore, the sample included two public research universities, one public two-year college, one graduate school, and one federal research center with college affiliations. This selected sample exhibited some institutional diversity, but still left out other perspectives such as those from private colleges and universities as well as those from for-profit postsecondary institutions. Additionally, this study obtained data from a single EMAP-certified university (i.e., Idaho State University) to serve as a blue light (i.e., a beacon example representing what an operational safety plan should look like for public safety) (BeaconMaster, 2018). There are eight institutions that hold EMAP certification in emergency planning and ISU was the second university in the country to obtain this accreditation. It would have strengthened the overall diversity of this study if more EMAP-certified institutions could have been included, especially Virginia Tech given its geographic proximity to the other selected institutions in Virginia as well as its status as the first higher education institution in the nation to obtain the EMAP accreditation. Another limitation of this study was the utilization of purposeful sampling, which within the context of qualitative research does present certain threats of credibility and trustworthiness. Since the primary data collection method was document analysis, findings were supplemented with interviews in which emergency management personnel from the selected five institutions had the opportunity to further explicate the operational safety plan process at their respective college or university. Once transcription and coding analysis were complete, the aforementioned threats to credibility and trustworthiness were mitigated through negative case analysis comparing differences between the EMAP-certified blue light institution and the non-EMAP certified institutions, member checking to clarify points made by informants and then memoing to bracket out researcher biases (Creswell, 2013). Finally, independent of the researcher and during initial data analysis, an outside individual with qualitative coding experience reviewed results and concurred with the researcher's findings.

INTERVIEW PROTOCOL FOR QUALITATIVE STUDIES

Interviewer: Hello, my name is Antonio Passaro, Jr., and I am an Old Dominion University (ODU) graduate student working on dissertation research exploring guiding principles, implementation factors, and candidate "best practices" when designing higher education operational safety plans. I appreciate very much your agreeing to let me ask you a few questions today about this topic. Since this is a research study, I am required to let you know that there are no right or wrong answers to any of my questions (I am interested in individual perspectives on and unique experiences with this topic) and I may ask follow-up questions for clarification if I do not understand something. Additionally, you can decide not to answer any question or decide to stop the interview at any time. Finally, under the Old Dominion University (ODU) Regulations for Social Science Studies, all answers are confidential and they will not be used outside of this research.

Before we get started, do I have your permission to record this interview?

Interviewee: _____
[Note: At this point, I would have had the subject(s) sign and return the informed consent form.]
[Start recording the interview]

Interviewer: OK, my name is Antonio Passaro, Jr. Today's date is _____, and the time is _____. I am here at _____ to interview _____.

1. Interviewer: Once again, thank you for participating in this interview. I would like to start by asking you to share a little bit about your professional background and current position?

   Interviewee: . . . . .

2. Interviewer: What is your role in the development, implementation, and changes/enhancement (i.e., updates) for your institution's operational safety plan(s)?

   Interviewee: . . . . .

3. Interviewer: When you are called upon during an emergency situation, what does a college emergency response plan expect of you? (Ask them to elaborate if need be)

   Interviewee: . . . . .

4. Interviewer: In looking at your operational safety plan, what principles did you and your team use to guide the development of this document(s) for your institution?

   Interviewee: . . . . .

5. Interviewer: In looking at your operational safety plan, what political/legal, financial, operational, and/or other factors do you and your team need to consider when implementing this document(s) in response to crisis?

   Interviewee: . . . . .

6. Interviewer: In reviewing your operational safety plan after a crisis, what design principles and/or implementation factors were not considered (i.e., lessons learned) in your plan?

   Interviewee: . . . . .

7. Interviewer: If you were to advise a peer at another institution regarding design principles and implementation factors, what practices would you propose should be highly considered in the design and implementation factors of their operational safety plan?

   Interviewee: . . . . .

8. Interviewer: OK, thank you very much. Your input is really useful and I appreciate the time that you allotted for this interview. May I contact you again (probably by email) if I have more questions or need clarifications for the issues we discussed?

   Interviewee: . . . . .

Interviewer: Thank you very much. [Stop recording and end interview]

Appendix C

Informed Consent Form

An Investigative Case Study Regarding the Design and Implementation of Operational Safety Plans for Crises at Colleges, Universities, and Affiliated Institutions

The Department of Higher Education Leadership at Old Dominion University (ODU) is committed to the highest standards of academic and research integrity. The following information is provided to your institution for the purpose of deciding whether or not to officially associate with the study's findings. You should be aware that even if you do not agree to endorse this project, your institution's identity will remain confidential.

The purpose of this research study is to discover guiding principles, implementation factors, and best practices associated with the design and implementation of operational safety plans at colleges, universities, and affiliated institutions. This study will include several case studies involving representative higher education and research institutions in the Commonwealth of Virginia. This researcher's objective is to advance understanding of the most effective and salient strategies associated with operational safety plans as well as critical design and implementation factors. I am asking for permission to explicitly identify guiding principles and best practices used by your institution for crisis and emergency management planning. Your institution does not have to prepare anything beyond the operational safety plans that are publicly available on your website or from your campus safety office.

Your consent to be identified in this study is solicited, but strictly voluntary. I assure you that, if your institution chooses not to be identified, its name would not be associated in any way with the research findings. In that instance, only a pseudonym will identify this institution.

If you would like additional information concerning this project before, during, or after it is complete, then please feel free to contact me by phone or email.

Sincerely,
Antonio Passaro, Jr.—Investigator
Old Dominion University (ODU)

_____ Dr. Dennis Gregory, Associate Professor-Educational Foundations & Leadership

Signature of administrator agreeing to their institution being identified (with my signature I affirm that I have the authority to grant this permission). Please sign on the line that is your institution's choice.

_____ Our institution is willing to be identified in the study.

_____ Our institution does not wish to be identified in the study.

Appendix D

Informed and Voluntary Consent Form

A Multiple Case Study Investigating Principles of Design and Implementation of Operational Safety Plans for Crises at Colleges, Universities, and Affiliated Institutions

The Department of Higher Education Leadership at Old Dominion University (ODU) supports the practice of protection for human subjects participating in research. The following information is provided for you to decide whether you wish to participate in the present study. You should be aware that even if you agree to participate, you are free to withdraw at any time without penalty.

I am interested in researching the strategies and components that members of college emergency management teams use in the design and implementation of operational safety plans. I am asking volunteers to participate in one twenty (20) minute qualitative follow-up interview (one-on-one) after document analysis of your institution's operational safety plans. The interview will involve a few questions about your background, your role in responding to an organizational emergency, and the process by which changes might be made to the institution's operational safety plan. You would not need to prepare anything for this interview. This interview is being conducted for the purpose of a class project. The Responsible Project Investigator is Dr. Dennis Gregory, Old Dominion University, Darden School of Education.

Your participation in any part of the study is solicited, but strictly voluntary. If you decide to participate in this study, then you may face a risk of mental or emotional discomfort when answering questions related to describing an actual emergency that you were involved in. The researcher tried to reduce these risks by providing ongoing consent reminders and carefully framed data collection methods. The main benefit to your participation in this study will be to shed light on how members of college communities design and implement operational safety plans, which will inform future research.

I assure you that your name will not be associated in any way with the research findings. Only a code number or pseudonym will identify this information. Notes, recordings, and transcriptions will be stored in a double-password protected environment. The results of this study may be used in

149

reports, but the researcher will not identify you. Any quotes will be scrubbed of contextual clues that may reveal the identity of the speaker(s) to readers.

If you choose to not be in the study, then that will in no way affect your future activities at the college and no one will know whether you chose to participate in the qualitative interview or not. The researcher is not providing payment or other inducements for participating in this study.

By signing this form, you are saying several things. You are saying that you have read and understand this form, the study, risks and benefits. If you would like additional information concerning this project before or after it is complete, then please feel free to contact the investigator (Antonio Passaro, Jr. or the P.I. (Dr. Dennis E. Gregory, Associate Professor of Higher Education). If at any time you feel pressured to participate, contact Dr. Laura Chezan, the current chair of Old Dominion University Darden College of Education and Professional Studies.

Subject's Printed Name & Signature: _____

Date: _____

Bibliography

Albiges, M. (2018). Preparing for hurricane Florence only cost Virginia $10.8M, thanks to FEMA picking up 75 percent of the bill. Retrieved from https://pilotonline.com/news/government/virginia/article_a44261be-d0a2-11e8-8f83-0311aad12b71.html.

Altheide, D. L., & Schneider, C. J. (2017). *Qualitative media analysis* (2nd ed.). Thousand Oaks, CA: Sage.

Asmussen, K. J., & Creswell, J. W. (2013). A Case Study—"Campus Response to a Student Gunman." In J. W. Creswell (Ed.), *Qualitative Inquiry and Research Design* (3rd ed., pp. 399–416). Los Angeles, CA: SAGE.

Baker, K., & Boland, K. (2011). Assessing Safety: A campus-wide initiative. *College Student Journal, 45*(4), 683–699.

Baldridge, J. V., Curtis, D. V., Ecker, G. P., & Riley, G. L. (1977). Alternative models of governance in higher education. In G. L. Riley & J. V. Baldridge (Eds.), *Governing Academic Organizations: New Problems, New Perspectives* (pp. 128–142). Berkeley, CA: McCutchan Publishing Corporation.

Barr, M. J., & McClellan, G. S. (2017). *Budgets and financial management in highereducation.* San Francisco, CA: Jossey-Bass.

Barron, G., & Yechiam, E. (2009). The coexistence of overestimation and underweighting of rare events and the contingent recency effect. *Judgement and decision making, 4*(6), 447–460.

Basken, P. (2015). Quakes rattle Oklahoma, exposing concerns about the flagship's control of state's seismologist. Retrieved from https://www.chronicle.com/article/Quakes-Rattle-Oklahoma/228563.

Bataille, G. M., & Cordova, D. I. (2014). Introduction. In G. M. Bataille and D. I. Cordova (Eds.), *Managing the unthinkable: Crisis preparation and responsefor campus leaders* (pp. 1–3). Sterling, VA: Stylus Publishing, LLC.

Bauman, D. (2017). How a defense dept. program equips campus police forces. *The Chronicle of Higher Education*. Retrieved from https://www-chronicle-com.proxy.lib.odu.edu/article/How-a-Defense-Dept-Program/241790.

BeaconMaster (2018). The importance of beacons in public safety. Published by BeaconMaster. Retrieved from http://beaconmaster.uk/2018/08/06/the-importance -of-beacons-in-public-safety/.

Becker, S. M. (2004). Emergency communication and information issues in terrorist events involving radioactive materials. *Biosecurity and Bioterrorism: Biodefense Strategy, Practice, and Science, 2*(3), 195–207.

Berg, B. L. (2001). *Qualitative research methods for the social sciences.* (4th ed.). Boston, MA: Allyn & Bacon.

Bertrand, N., & Sevens M. (2020). From distraction to disaster: How Coronavirus crept up on Washington. Retrieved from https://www.politico.com /news/2020/03/30/how-coronavirus-shook-congress-complacency-155058.

Blair, J. P., & Martaindale, M. H. (2013). *United States active shooter events from 2000 to 2010: Training and equipment implications.* San Marcos, TX: Advanced law enforcement rapid response training (ALERRT).

Blair, J. P., Nichols, T., Burns, D., & Curnutt, J. R. (2013). *Active shooter: Events and responses.* Boca Raton, FL: CRC Press.

Blair, J. P., & Schweit, K. W. (2014). *A study of active shooter incidents, 2000–2013.* Washington, DC: Texas State University and U.S. Department of Justice, Federal Bureau of Investigation.

Blanchard, J. & Baez, B. (2016). The legal environment: The implementation of legal change on campus. In M. N. Bastedo, P. G. Altbach & P. J. Gumport (Eds.), *American Higher Education in the Twenty-First Century: Social, Political, and Economic Challenges* (4th ed., pp. 281–309). Baltimore, MD: The John Hopkins University Press.

Bogdan, R., & Biklen, S. (2007). *Qualitative research for education: An introduction to theory and practice* (5th ed.). New York, NY: Pearson Education, Inc.

Boin, A., Hart, P., Stern, E., & Sundelius, B. (2005). *The politics of crisis management: Public leadership under pressure.* New York, NY: Cambridge University Press.

Bonanno, C. M., & Levenson, R. L. (2014). School shooters: history, current theoretical and empirical findings, and strategies for prevention. *SAGE Open, 4*(1), 1–11.

Booker, L. (2014). Crisis management: Changing times for colleges. *Journal of College Admission,* 16–23.

Bowen, G. A. (2009). Document analysis as a qualitative research method. *Qualitative research journal, 9*(2), 27–40.

Bowen, W. G. (2013). *Higher education in the digital age.* New York, NY: Ithaka Princeton university press.

Braga, A. A., & Clarke, R. V. (2014). Explaining high-risk concentrations of crime in the city: Social disorganization, crime opportunities, and important next steps. *Journal of Research in Crime and Delinquency, 51*(4), 480–498.

Braithwaite, J. (1975). Population growth and crime. *Australia & New Zealand Journal of Criminology, 8*(1), 57–60.

Brinsfield, K. H., & Mitchell, Jr., E. (2015). The department of homeland security's role in enhancing and implementing the response to active shooter and intentional mass casualty events. *American College of Surgeons Bulletin, 100*(1S), 24–26.

Briggs, T. W., & Kennedy, W. G. (2016). Active shooter: An agent-based model of unarmed resistance, *2016 Winter Simulation Conference*, Arlington, VA, December 11–14, 2016. Piscataway, NJ: IEEE Press.

Bryman, A. (2012) *Social research methods*. 4th ed. Oxford: Oxford University Press.

Bunge, J. (2021). JBS paid $11 million to resolve ransomware attack. Retrieved from: https://www.wsj.com/articles/jbs-paid-11-million-to-resolve-ransomware -attack-11623280781.

Code of Virginia, 23.1-804 (effective July 1, 2020).

Code of Virginia, 23.1-805 (effective October 1, 2016).

Code of Virginia, 23.9.2:10 (effective March 7, 2008).

Cohen, A. M., Brawer, F. B., & Kisker, C. B. (2014). *The American community college*. 6th edition. San Fransisco, CA: Jossey-Bass.

Committee on the judiciary House of Representatives. (2019). The impeachment inquiry into President Donald J. Trump: Constitutional grounds for presidential impeachment. Retrieved from: https://www.govinfo.gov/content/pkg/CHRG -116hhrg38933/html/CHRG-116hhrg38933.htm

Conrad, C.D., Galea, L.A.M., Kuroda, Y., & McEwen, B.S. (1996). Chronic stress impairs rat spatial memory on the Y maze and this effect is blocked by tianeptine pretreatment. *Behavioral neuroscience, 110*(6), 1321–1334.

Cooper, C. & Block, R. (2006). *Disaster: Hurricane Katrina and the failure of homeland security*. New York, NY: Times Books.

Cornish, D. B., & Clarke, R. V. (1986). *The reasoning criminal: Rational choice perspectives on offending*. New York, NY: Springer-Verlag.

Cortright, E. M. (1970). Report of Apollo 13 review board. National aeronautics and space administration Apollo 13 review board. Retrieved from https://history.nasa .gov/ap13cortright.pdf.

Cowen, S., & Seifter, B. (2018). *Winnebagos on Wednesdays: How visionary leadership can transform higher education*. Princeton, NJ: Princeton University Press.

Creswell, J. W. (2013). *Qualitative inquiry & research design: Choosing among five approaches*. 3rd edition. Thousand Oaks, CA: Sage.

Creswell, J.W., & Plano Clark, V. L. (2011). *Designing and conducting mixed methods research* (2nd Edition). Thousand Oaks, CA: Sage.

Criminal Justice. (2019). Rational choice theory. Retrieved from http://criminal -justice.iresearchnet.com/criminology/theories/rational-choice-theory/.

Dahl, P. P., Bonham, Jr., G., & Reddington, F. P. (2016). Community college faculty: Attitudes toward guns on campus. *Community College Journal of Research and Practice, 40*(8), 706–717.

De Domenico, M., Ghorbani, M. A., Makarynskyy, O., Makarynska, D., & Asadi. (2013). Chaos and reproduction in sea level. *Applied Mathematical Modelling, 37*, 3687–3697.

Dede, C., Ketelhut, D.J., Whitehouse, P., Breit, L., and McCloskey, E.M. (2009). A Research Agenda for Online Teacher Professional Development. *Journal of Teacher Education, 60*(1), 8–19.

Deisinger, E. R. D., & Scalora, M. J. (2016). Threat assessment and management in higher education in the United States: A review of the 10 years since the mass casualty incident at Virginia Tech. *Journal of Threat Assessment and management, 3*(3–4), 186–199.

Denham, M. A., & Khemka, A. K. (2018). Homeland security and emergency management in institutions of higher education (IHE): Texas case study. In C. A. Brebbia (Ed.), *Disaster management* (pp. 229–241). Southampton, UK: WIT Press.

Dietz, D. (2017). UCC shooting instructed UO on how to respond to disaster. Retrieved from http://www.registerguard.com/rg/news/local/35191619-75/ucc-shooting-instructed-uo-on-how-to-respond-to-disaster.html.csp.

Donald, J. G. (2009). The commons: Disciplinary and interdisciplinary encounters. In C. Kreber (Ed.), *The university and its disciplines: Teaching and learning within and beyond disciplinary boundaries*, (pp. 35–49). New York, NY: Routledge.

Dow, K., & Cutter, S. L. (2000). Public orders and personal opinions: household strategies for hurricane risk assessment. *Environmental hazards, 2*, 143–155.

Dumoulin, J. (2001). Apollo-13 (29). Kennedy Space Center. Retrieved from https://science.ksc.nasa.gov/history/apollo/apollo-13/apollo-13.html.

Duryea, E. D. (2000). Evolution of university organization. In C. M. Brown (Ed.), *Organization and governance in higher education* (pp. 3–15). 5th ed. New York, NY: Pearson Custom Publishing.

Eastern Virginia Medical School (EVMS). (2017). Emergency operations plan. Norfolk, VA: Eastern Virginia Medical School.

Eells, G. T., & Rockland-Miller, H. S. (2011). Assessing and responding to disturbed and disturbing students: Understanding the role of administrative teams in institutions of higher education. *Journal of College Student Psychotherapy, 25*, 8–23.

Emergency Management Accreditation Program (EMAP). (2016). 2016 Emergency management standard. Emergency Management Accreditation Program. Retrieved from https://www.emap.org/index.php/root/about-emap/96-emap-em-4-2016/file.

Emergency Management Accreditation Program (EMAP). (2019). Emergency management accreditation program overview. Emergency Management Accreditation Program. https://emap.org.

Evans, T. M., Bira, L., Gastelum, J. B., Weiss, L. T., & Vanderford, N. L. (2018).

EveryTown for gun safety. (2018). Gunfire on school grounds in the United States. Retrieved from https://everytownresearch.org/gunfire-in-school/.

Evidence for mental health crisis in graduate education. *Nature Biotechnology, 36*(3), 282–284.

Federal Emergency Management Agency [FEMA]. (2011a). *Fundamentals of emergency management*. Scotts Valley, CA: CreateSpace Independent Publishing Platform.

Federal Emergency Management Agency. (2011b). National disaster recovery framework: Strengthening disaster recovery for the nation. Federal Emergency Management Agency. Retrieved from https://www.fema.gov/pdf/recoveryframework/ndrf.pdf.

Federal Emergency Management Agency. (2012). Operational templates and guidance for EMS mass incident deployment. Federal Emergency Management

Agency. Retrieved from https://www.usfa.fema.gov/downloads/pdf/publications /templates_guidance_ems_mass_incident_deployment.pdf.

Federal Emergency Management Agency. (2015). Effective coordination of recovery resources for state, tribal, territorial and local incident. Federal Emergency Management Agency. Retrieved from https://www.fema.gov/media-library -data/1423604728233-1d76a43cabf1209678054c0828bbe8b8/EffectiveCoordina tionofRecoveryResourcesGuide020515vFNL.pdf.

Federal Student Aid. (2018). Clery act reports. Retrieved from https://studentaid .ed.gov/sa/about/data-center/school/clery-act-reports.

Fish, S. (1989). Being interdisciplinary is so very hard to do. *Profession,* 15–22.

Flack, E. (2017). 12 years after Hurricane Katrina, FEMA asks survivor for $12k back. WTSP. Retrieved from https://www.wtsp.com/article/news/12-years-after -hurricane-katrina-fema-asks-survivor-for-12k-back/480611234.

Ford, J. L., & Frei, S. S. (2016). Training for the unthinkable: Examining message characteristics on motivations to engage in an active-shooter response video. *Communication Studies, 67*(4), 438–454.

Fox, J. A., & Savage, J. (2009). Mass murder goes to college: An examination of changes on college campus following Virginia Tech. *American Behavioral Scientist, 52*(10), 1465–1485.

Fox, J. A., & Levin, J. (2015). Mass confusion concerning mass murder. *The Criminologist, 40*(1), 8–11.

Gittleson, Ben. (2020). Trump admitted he deliberately played down coronavirus threat: Reports. Retrieved from: https://abcnews.go.com/Politics/trump-admitted -deliberately-played-coronavirus-threat-reports/story?id=72904348.

Glassman, R. B. (1973). Persistence and loose coupling in living systems. *Behavioral Science, 18*, 83–98.

Gleick, J. (2008). *Chaos: Making a new science.* New York, NY: Penguin Books.

Grasmick, H. G., & Bursik, R. J., Jr. (1990). Conscience, significant others, and rational choice: Extending the deterrence model. *Law & Society Review, 24*, 837–862.

Grasmick, Harold G., Robert J. Bursik, Jr., and Bruce J. Arneklev. (1993). Reduction in Drunk Driving as a Response to Increased Threats of Shame, Embarrassment, and Legal Sanctions. *Criminology, 31,* 41–67.

Gregory, D. E., & Janosik, S. M. (2002). The Clery Act: How effective is it? Perceptions from the field—the current state of the research and recommendations for improvement. *Stetson Law Review, XXXII,* 7–59.

Griffin, O. R. (2009). Confronting the evolving safety and security challenges at colleges and universities. *University of New Hampshire law review, 5*(3), 413–432.

Harrison, D. F. (2014). Levels of crises and leadership responses: Role differentiation and collaboration. In G. M. Bataille & D. I. Cordova, *Managing the unthinkable: Crisis preparation and response for campus leaders.* Sterling, VA: Stylus.

Haselton, M. G., Nettle, D., & Murray, D. R. (2015). The evolution of cognitive bias. In D. M. Buss (Ed.), *The handbook of evolutionary psychology Volume 2: Integrations* (2nd ed., pp. 968–987). Hoboken, NJ: John Wiley & Sons, Inc.

Hill, G., & Hill, K. (2018a). Duty of care. Retrieved from https://dictionary.law.com /Default.aspx?selected=599.

Hill, G., & Hill, K. (2018b). In Loco Parentis. Retrieved from https://dictionary.law
.com/Default.aspx?selected=968.

Hill, G., & Hill, K. (2018c). Tort. Retrieved from http://dictionary.law.com/Default
.aspx?selected=2137.

Hoover, E. (2008). Louisiana shootings underscore vulnerability of open campuses.
The Chronicle of Higher Education, 54(24), A17.

Hughes, S., White, R. J., & Hertz, G. (2008). A new technique for mitigating risk on
US college campuses. *Journal of higher education policy and management, 30*(3),
309–318.

Hutchison, E.D. (2015). *Dimensions of human behavior: person and environment.*
Thousand Oaks, CA: Sage.

Hyman, I .E., Wulff, A. N., Thomas, A. K. (2018). Crime blindness: How selective attention and inattentional blindness can disrupt eyewitness awareness and memory.
Policy insights from behavioral and brain science, 5(2), 202–208.

Idaho State University (ISU) (2019). Emergency Operations Plan. Pocatello, ID:
Idaho State University.

Idaho State University (ISU) (2018a). Resource and emergency response gap analysis. Pocatello, ID: Idaho State University.

Idaho State University (ISU) (2018b). Strategic plan FY2018–FY2022. ISU.
Retrieved from https://isu.edu/media/top-level/about-us/08-ISU-Strategic-Plan
-2018-2022-SBOE-V2-5-10-2017.pdf.

Indiana University (IU). (2018). Bomb threat overview. IU. Retrieved from https://
protect.iu.edu/emergency-planning/procedures/bomb-threats.html.

Inskeep, S. (2019). Is climate change contributing to slower moving hurricanes? National Public Radio. Retrieved from https://www.npr.org/2019/09/04/757394753
/is-climate-change-contributing-to-slower-moving-hurricanes.

International Association of Emergency Managers (2007). Principles of emergency
management supplement Retrieved from https://www.iaem.com/documents/Prin
ciples-of-Emergency-Management-Supplement.pdf.

Janosik, S. M., & Gregory, D. E. (2003). The Clery Act and its influence on campus
law enforcement practices. *NASPA Journal, 41*(1), 182–199.

Jennings, W. G., Gover, A., & Pudrzynska, D. (2007). Are institutions of higher learning safe? A descriptive study of campus safety issues and self-reported campus
victimization among male and female college students. *Journal of Criminal Justice
Education, 18*(2), 191–208.

Johns, L., & Jarvis, J. P. (2016). Leadership during crisis response: Challenges and
evolving research. FBI Law Enforcement Bulletin (LEB). Retrieved from https://
leb.fbi.gov/articles/featured-articles/leadership-during-crisis-response-challenges
-and-evolving-research.

Johnson, G. S., & Rainey, S. A. (2007). Hurricane Katrina impacts on three historically black colleges and universities (HBCUs): Voices from displaced students.
Race, gender & class, 14(1/2), 100–119.

Johnson, J. (2012). Report: Virginia Tech massacre cost $48.2 million. The
Washington Post. Retrieved from https://www.washingtonpost.com/blogs/campus

-overload/post/report-virginia-tech-massacre-cost-482-million/2012/04/13/gIQAd DmxET_blog.html.

Johnstone, D. B. (2016). Financing American higher education: Reconciling institutional financial viability and student affordability. In M. N. Bastedo, P. G. Altbach, & P. J. Gumport (Eds.), *American Higher Education in the Twenty-First Century: Social, Political, and Economic Challenges* (4th ed., pp. 310–341). Baltimore, MD: The John Hopkins University Press.

Kaarbo, J., & Beasley, R. K. (1999). A practical guide to the comparative case study method in political psychology. *Political Psychology, 20*(2), 369–391.

Kaminski, R. J., Koons-Witt, K., Thompson, N. S., & Weiss, D. (2010). The impacts of the Virginia Tech and northern Illinois university shootings on fear of crime on campus. *Journal of criminal justice* (38), 88–98.

Kappeler, V. E., & Kraska, P. B. (2013). Normalising police militarization, living in denial. *Policing and Society, 25*(3), 268–275.

Karlin, L. (2007). FEMA asks students to return Hurricane Katrina aid. *The New York Times*. Retrieved from https://archive.nytimes.com/www.nytimes.com/uwire /uwire_FHDW021320074274522.html.

Kealy, S. J. (2003). Reexamining the Posse Comitatus act: Toward a right to civil law enforcement. *Yale Law & policy review, 21*(2), 383–442.

Kierkegaard, S. (1843). *Journalen.* Retrieved from http://homepage.divms.uiowa .edu/~jorgen/kierkegaardquotesource.html

Knight, V. (2020). Obama team left pandemic playbook for Trump administration, officials confirm. Retrieved from https://www.pbs.org/newshour/nation/obama -team-left-pandemic-playbook-for-trump-administration-officials-confirm.

Kornell, N., & Bjork, R. A. (2009). A stability bias in human memory: Overestimating remembering and underestimating learning. *Journal of Experimental Psychology, 138*(4), 449–468.

Kraska, P. B. (2007). Militarization and policing—Its relevance to 21st century police. Policing: *A Journal of Policy and Practice, 1*(4), 501–513.

Kraska, P. B., & Kappeler, V. E. (1997). Militarizing American police: The rise and normalization of paramilitary units. *Social Problems, 44*(1), 1–18.

Krathwohl, D. R. (2004). *Methods of educational and social science research: An integrated approach.* 2nd Edition. Long Grove, IL: Waveland Press, Inc.

Kubrin, C. E., Stucky, T. D., & Krohn, M. D. (2009). *Researching theories of crime and deviance.* New York, NY: Oxford University Press.

Lannon, Jr., P. G. (2014). Direct Threat and Caring for Students at Risk for Self-Harm: Where We Stand Now. National Association of College and University Attorneys (NACUA) *Notes, 12*(8), 1–15.

Lawrence, P. R., & Lorsch, J. W. (1967). Differentiation and integration in complex organizations. *Administrative Science Quarterly, 12*(1), 1–47.

Lee, P. (2011). The curious life of *in loco parentis* at American universities. *Higher education in review, 8,* 65–90.

LegalMatch. (2018). Tort law liability. Retrieved from https://www.legalmatch.com /law-library/article/tort-law-liability.html.

Lincoln, Y. S. (2009). "What a long, strange trip it's been . . .": Twenty-five of qualitative and new paradigm research. *Qualitative inquiry, 16*(1), 3–9.

Lincoln, Y. S., & Guba, E. G. (1985). *Naturalistic Inquiry*. Newbury Park, CA: Sage Publications.

Lipka, S. (2007). The price of inaction: *Chronicle of higher education, 53*(47), 20.

Lipka, S. (2008). 28 families reach final settlements with Virginia tech and the state. Retrieved from https://www.chronicle.com/article/28-Families-Reach-Final/908.

Loftus, E. F. (2019). Eyewitness testimony. *Applied cognitive psychology, 33*, 498–503.

Loh, J. (2013) Inquiry into issues of trustworthiness and quality in narrative studies: A perspective. *The qualitative report, 18*(65), 1–15.

Ludlam, F. H. (1948). The forms of ice-clouds. *Quarterly Journal of the Royal Meteorological Society, 74*(319), 39–56.

Luhman, J. T., & Cunliffe, A. L. (2013). Key concepts in Organization Theory. Thousand Oaks, CA: Sage Publications Inc.

Luttrell, M., & Wasserman, A. (2014). Marcus Luttrell, former navy seal and author of lone survivor, speaks to buckeyes: Ohio state spring football 2014. *Ohio State*. Retrieved from https://www.cleveland.com/osu/2014/03/marcus_luttrell_former _navy_se.html.

Mackey, J. L. (1995). Fractals or fish: Does a space for interdisciplinarity exists? *Issues in Integrative Studies, 13*, 101–113.

Mahaffie, L. B. (2014). *Implementation of changes to the Clery act made by the violence against women reauthorization act of 2013 (VAWA)*. Washington, DC: U.S. department of education office of postsecondary education.

Mandelbrot, B. B. (1982). *The fractal geometry of nature*. New York, NY: Times Books.

March, J. G. (1981). Footnotes to organization change. *Administrative Science Quarterly, 26*(4), 563–577.

Mason, S. (2014). Rising waters and campus renewal: Leading the University of Iowa through and beyond the flood of 2008. In G. M. Bataille and D. I. Cordova (Eds.), *Managing the unthinkable: Crisis preparation and response for campus leaders* (pp. 61–73). Sterling, VA: Stylus Publishing, LLC.

Maxwell, J. A. (2005). *Qualitative research design: An interactive approach*. 2nd edition. Thousand Oaks, CA: Sage Publications, Inc.

Monahan, T. (2010). The future of security? Surveillance operations at Homeland Security fusion centers. *Social Justice, 37*(2), 84–98.

Mumper, M., Gladieux, L. E., King, J. E., & Corrigan, M. E. (2016). The Federal Government and Higher Education. In M. N. Bastedo, P. G. Altbach & P. J. Gumport (Eds.), *American Higher Education in the Twenty-First Century: Social, Political, and Economic Challenges* (4th ed., pp. 212–237). Baltimore, MD: The John Hopkins University Press.

Myers, B., & Lusk, E. (2017). Rising waters, threatened campuses. Retrieved from https://www.chronicle.com/interactives/rising-threat.

NASA. (2009). Apollo 13. NASA. Retrieved from https://www.nasa.gov/mission _pages/apollo/missions/apollo13.html.

NASA. (2015). Emergency Management Plan (EMP). Hampton, VA: NASA.

NASA Jet Propulsion Laboratory. (2019). Global climate change: Vital signs of the planet. California Institute of Technology. Retrieved from https://climate.nasa.gov/.

National Center for Campus Public Safety. (2016a). Emerging issues in managing international programs at institutions of higher education. National Center for Campus Public Safety. Retrieved from https://www.nccpsafety.org/assets/files /library/NCCPS_Global_Issues_Report_052416.pdf.

National Center for Campus Public Safety. (2016b). National higher education emergency management program needs assessment. National Center for Campus Public Safety. Retrieved from https://www.nccpsafety.org/assets/files/library /NCCPS_EM_Needs_Assessment_FINAL_113016.pdf.

National Center for Education Statistics (NCES). (2020). College navigator. Retrieved from https://nces.ed.gov/collegenavigator/.

National Commission on Terrorist Attacks upon the United States. (2004). The 9/11 Commission Report. Washington, DC: National Commission on Terrorist Attacks upon the United States.

National Domestic Preparedness Consortium. (2018). Annual report FY 2018. National Domestic Preparedness Consortium. Retrieved from https://www.ndpc.us /pdf/2018_NDPC_AR.pdf.

National Law Enforcement and Corrections Technology Center. (2009). Early warning for campus emergencies. National Law Enforcement and Corrections Technology Center. Retrieved from https://www.nccpsafety.org/assets/files/library /Early_Warning_for_Campus_Emergencies.pdf.

National Weather Service. (2016). Hurricane Katrina—August 2005. *National Weather Service* retrieved from https://www.weather.gov/mob/katrina.

Nelson, M. D. (2014). Preparation, response, and recovery: The everydayness of crisis leadership. In G. M. Bataille and D. I. Cordova (Eds.), *Managing the unthinkable: Crisis preparation and response for campus leaders* (pp. 74–81). Sterling, VA: Stylus Publishing, LLC.

NOVA. (2008). Fractals: Hunting the hidden dimension. Retrieved from https://www .youtube.com/watch?v=HvXbQb57lsE.

Old Dominion University. (2018a). ODU Cares. ODU. Retrieved from https://www .odu.edu/success/resources/odu-cares.

Old Dominion University. (2018b). T.E.A.M. Threat education assessment & management. ODU. Retrieved from https://www.odu.edu/life/health-afety/safety/pro grams/team.

Old Dominion University. (2018c). ODU resilience collaborative. ODU. Retrieved from https://www.odu.edu/impact/initiatives/resiliencecollaborative.

Old Dominion University. (2019). Crisis and Emergency Management Plan. Norfolk, VA: Old Dominion University.

O'Leary, Z. (2014). *The essential guide to doing your research project* (2nd ed.). Thousand Oaks, CA: Sage.

Oliver, W. M. (2009). Policing for homeland security: Policy & research. *Criminal justice policy review, 20*(3), 253–260.

Ordonez, F. (2021). In wake of pipline hack, Biden signs executive order on cyber-security. Retrieved from: https://www.npr.org/2021/05/12/996355601/in-wake-of-pipeline-hack-biden-signs-executive-order-on-cybersecurity.

Orlikowski, W. J. (1992). "The duality of technology: Rethinking the concept of tech-nology in organizations," *Organization Science, 3*, 398–427.

Patton, R. C., & Gregory, D. E. (2014). Perceptions of safety by on-campus location, rurality, and type of security/police force: The case of the community college. *Journal of College Student Development, 55*(5), 451–460.

Paules, C. I., Eisinger, R. W., Marston, H. D., & Fauci, A. S. (2017). What recent history has taught us about responding to emergering infectious disease threats. Retrieved from: https://www.acpjournals.org/doi/full/10.7326/M17-2496?journal Code=aim&.

Poole, G. (2009). Academic disciplines: Homes or barricades. In C. Kreber (Ed.), *The university and its disciplines: Teaching and learning within and beyond disciplin-ary boundaries* (pp. 50–57). New York, NY: Routledge.

Porter, L. (2013). Trying something old: The impact of shame sanctioning on drunk driving and alcohol-related traffic safety. *Law & Social Inquiry, 38*(4), 863–891.

Randazzo, C., & Cameron, J. K. (2012). From presidential protection to campus se-curity: A brief history of threat assessment in North American schools and college. *Journal of college student psychotherapy, 26*, 277–290.

Randazzo, M. R., & Plummer, E. (2009). Implementing behavioral threat assessment on campus: A Virginia Tech demonstration project. Retrieved from: http://rems .ed.gov/docs/VT_ThreatAssessment09.pdf.

Rasmussen, C. (2019). Huge cavity in Antarctic glacier signals rapid decay. Retrieved from https://sealevel.nasa.gov/news/152/huge-cavity-in-antarctic-glacier-signals -rapid-decay.

Reynolds, B., & Seeger, M. W. (2005). Crisis and emergency risk communication as an integrative model. *Journal of Health Communication, 10*, 43–55.

Richardson, F. C. (1994). The president's role in shaping the culture of academic institutions. In J. D. Davis (Ed.), *Coloring the halls of ivy: Leadership & diversity in the academy.* Bolton, MA: Anker Publishing Company, Inc.

Rodgers, T. (2018). Update: Major hurricane Florence targets Carolina coastlines. *SNL Energy Power Daily.* Retrieved from https://www-proquest-com.proxy.lib .odu.edu/docview/2102631561/D75E82AD8F254C55PQ/35?accountid=12967

Roux-Dufort, C. (2007). Is crisis management (only) a management of exceptions? *Journal of Contingencies and Crisis Management, 15*(2), 105–114.

Saletan, W. (2020). Trump's excuse for his coronavirus lies is even more incrimi-nating: The "panic" defense is part of his collusion with China. Retrieved from: https://slate.com/news-and-politics/2020/09/trump-woodward-book-panic-corona virus-china.html.

Sapolsky, R. M. (1992). *Stress, the aging brain and the mechanisms of neuron death.* Cambridge, MA: MIT press.

Saraga, A. (2008). Supreme Court of New York Nassau County. *Bursac v. Suozzi, 26*(868 N.Y.S.2d 470 [Sup. Ct. Nassau County 2008]), 941–953.

Schafer, J. A., Heiple, E., Giblin, M. J., & Burruss, G. W. (2010). Critical incident preparedness and response on post-secondary campuses. *Journal of criminal justice, 38*(3), 311–317.

Scheidegger, A. E. (1997). Complexity theory of natural disasters; boundaries of self-structured domains. *Natural Hazards, 16,* 103–112.

Schildkraut, J. McKenna, J. M., & Elsass, H. J. (2017). Understanding crisis communications: Examining students' perceptions about campus notification systems. *Security journal, 30*(2), 605–620.

Scott, W.R., and Davis, G.F. (2007). *Organizations and organizing: Rational, natural, and open system perspectives.* Englewood Cliffs, NJ: Prentice Hall.

Seltzer, R. (2018). Jacksonville state campus closed after tornado. Retrieved from https://www.insidehighered.com/quicktakes/2018/03/22/jacksonville-state-campus-closed-after-tornado.

Shaban, H., Nakashima, E., & Lerman, R. (2021). JBS, world's biggest meat supplier, says its systems are coming back online after cyberattack shut down plants in U.S. Retrieved from https://www.washingtonpost.com/business/2021/06/01/jbs-cyberattack-meat-supply-chain/.

Sheldon, P. (2018). Emergency alert communications on college campuses: Understanding students' perceptions of the severity of a crisis and their intentions to share the alert with parents and friends. *Western journal of communication, 82*(1), 100–116.

Shenton, A. K. (2004). Strategies for ensuring trustworthiness in qualitative research projects. *Education for information, 22*(2), 63–75.

Smith, K. (2003). Five regions of Virginia: The Tidewater region. Retrieved from https://regionsofva.weebly.com/tidewater.html.

Stafford, D. (2014). What can you do to keep your campus from having to rebuild in the first place? In G. M. Bataille and D. I. Cordova (Eds.), *Managing the unthinkable: Crisis preparation and response for campus leaders* (pp. 47–58). Sterling, VA: Stylus Publishing, LLC.

Stahl, L. (2009). Eyewitness: How accurate is visual memory? CBS News 60 minutes. Retrieved from https://www.cbsnews.com/news/eyewitness-how-accurate-is-visual-memory/.

Stake, R. E. (2000). Case studies. In N. K. Denzen & Y. S. Lincoln (Eds.), *Handbook of qualitative research* (2nd ed.), pp. 435–454. Thousand Oaks, CA: Sage.

State Council of Higher Education for Virginia (SCHEV). (2019). Colleges and universities. SCHEV. Retrieved from https://www.schev.edu/index/students-and-parents/explore/virginia-institutions.

St. John, E. P., & Parsons, M. D. (Eds.). (2004). *Public funding of higher education: Changing contexts and new rationales.* Baltimore, MD: The Johns Hopkins university press.

Strauss, A., & Corbin, Jr. (1994). Grounded theory methodology: An overview. In N. K. Denzin & Y. S. Lincoln (Eds.), *Handbook of qualitative research* (pp. 273–285). Thousand Oaks, CA: Sage.

Strauss, A., & Corbin, J. (1998). *Basics of qualitative research: Technique and procedures for developing grounded theory* (2nd ed.). Thousand Oaks, CA: Sage.

Suen, H. K., Lei, P-W., & Li, H. (2012). Data analysis for effective decision making. In M. A. Bray & T. J. Kehle (Eds.), *Oxford Handbook of School Psychology* (pp. 140–168). New York, NY: Oxford University Press, Inc.

Sullenberger, C. (2009). *Highest duty: My search for what really matters*. New York, NY: Harper Collins Publishers.

Sutcliffe, K. (2018). Managing for the future: A commentary on crisis management research. In K. E. Weick & K. M. Sutcliffe (Eds.), *The Routledge Companion to Risk, Crisis and Emergency Management* (pp. 486–490). Abingdon, U.K.: Taylor and Francis.

Swinth, R. L. (1974). *Organizational systems for management: Designing, planning and implementation*. Columbus, OH: Grid.

Theodoulou, S. Z., & Kofinis, C. (2004). *The art of the game: Understanding American public policy making*. Belmont, CA: Wadsworth/Thomson Learning.

Thompson, A., Price, J. H., Mrdjenovich, A., J., & Khubchandani, J. (2009). Reducing firearm-related violence on college campuses—Police chiefs' perceptions and practices. *Journal of American college health, 58*(3), 247–254.

Tidewater Community College (TCC). (2017). Crisis and emergency management plan (CEMP). Norfolk, VA: Tidewater Community College.

Tonry, M., & Farrington, D. P. (1995). Strategic approaches to crime prevention. The *University of Chicago Press Journals, 19*, 1–20.

Traynor, P. (2012). Characterizing the security implications of third-party emergency alert systems over cellular text messaging services. *IEEE transactions on mobile computing, 11*(6), 983–994.

Turton, W., & Jacobs, J. (2021). Massive ransomware attack may impact thousands of victims. Retrieved from: https://www.bloomberg.com/news/articles/2021-07-03/number-of-victims-continues-to-grow-in-massive-ransomware-attack.

Turton, W., & Mehrotra, K. (2021). Hackers breached colonial pipeline using compromised password. Retrieved from: https://www.bloomberg.com/news/articles/2021-06-04/hackers-breached-colonial-pipeline-using-compromised-password.

United States Department of Education. (2007). *Eastern Michigan university program review report*. Denver, CO: Federal student aid school participation team-Denver.

United States Department of Education. (2018). Family educational rights and privacy act (FERPA). Retrieved from https://www2.ed.gov/policy/gen/guid/fpco/ferpa/index.html.

United States Department of Health and Human Services Office of Inspector General (2019). Emergency response. U.S. Department of Health and Human Services. Retrieved from https://oig.hhs.gov/reports-and-publications/featured-topics/emergency/.

United States Department of Homeland Security. (2006). A performance review of FEMA'S disaster management activities in response to hurricane Katrina. Retrieved from https://www.oig.dhs.gov/assets/Mgmt/OIG_06-32_Mar06.pdf.

United States Department of Homeland Security. (2014). National emergency communications plan. Department of Homeland Security. Retrieved from https://www.dhs.gov/sites/default/files/publications/2014%20National%20Emergency%20Communications%20Plan_October%2029%202014_0.pdf.

United States Department of Homeland Security. (2018). Crisis event response and recovery access (CERRA) framework: An emergency preparedness access implementation and best practice guide. Department of Homeland Security. Retrieved from https://www.dhs.gov/sites/default/files/publications/Crisis%20 Event%20Response%20and%20Recovery%20Access%20%28CERRA%29%20 Framework.pdf.

United States Department of Justice FBI. (2016). Making prevention a reality: Identifying, assessing, and managing the threat of targeted attacks. Department of Justice FBI. Retrieved from https://www.fbi.gov/file-repository/making-prevention-a -reality.pdf/view.

United States Department of Justice. (2018). Overview of title IX of the education amendments of 1972, 20 U.S.C. A§ 1681 ET. SEQ. Retrieved from https://www .justice.gov/crt/overview-title-ix-education-amendments-1972-20-usc-1681-et-seq.

United States Department of Justice Civil Rights Division. (2018). Information and technical assistance on the Americans with disabilities Act. Retrieved from https:// www.ada.gov/ada_intro.htm.

United States Government Accountability Office (GAO). (2018). Emergency management: Federal agencies could improve dissemination of resources to colleges. Washington D.C.: U.S. Department Accountability Office.

University of California—Irvine (UC Irvine). (2017). Emergency Operations Plan. Retrieved from http://www.police.uci.edu/em/EmergencyManagementPlan.pdf.

University of Rhode Island (URI). (2015). Hurricanes: Science and society, hurricane movement. Retrieved from http://www.hurricanescience.org/science/science/hur ricanemovement/.

U.S. Department of Agriculture (USDA). (2020). IACUC protocol review. National Agricultural library. Retrieved from https://www.nal.usda.gov/awic/iacuc-proto col-review.

U.S. Senate Committee on Health, Education Labor & Pensions. (2020). Senate health committee announces brifing to update senators on coronavirus. Retrieved from: https://www.help.senate.gov/chair/newsroom/press/senate-health-commit tee-announces-briefing-to-update-senators-on-coronavirus.

van der Vegt, G. S., Essens, P., Wahlstrom, M., & George, G. (2015). Managing risk and resilience. *Academy of Management Journal, 58*(4), 971–980.

van Heerden, I., & Bryan, M. (2006). *The storm: What went wrong and why during Hurricane Katrina.* New York, NY: Penguin Group.

Veal, A. J. (2011) *Research methods for leisure and tourism.* 4th ed. England: Pearson Education Limited.

Veenema, T. G., Walden, B, Feinstein, N., & Williams, J. P. (2008). Factors affecting hospital-based nurses' willingness to respond to a radiation emergency. *Disaster Medicine and Public Health Preparedness, 2*(4), 224–229.

Vervaele, J. A. E. (2005). Terrorism and information sharing between the intelligence and law enforcement communities in the U.S. and the Netherlands: Emergency criminal law? *Revue internationale de droit pénal, 76*, 409–443.

Virginia Center for School and Campus Safety (VCSCS). (2016). Final report on threat assessment teams in Virginia institutions of higher education: Survey of

Practices (2013–2014). Retrieved from https://www.dcjs.virginia.gov/sites/dcjs .virginia.gov/files/publications/research/final-report-threat-assessment-teams-vir ginia-institutions-higher-education-2013-2014.pdf.

Virginia Department of Criminal Justice Services (DCJS) (2020). Certification process and mandated in-service requirements-law enforcement officer. Virginia Department of Criminal Justice Services. Retrieved from https://www .dcjs.virginia.gov/law-enforcement/certification-process-and-mandated-service -requirements-le-officer.

Virginia Tech Emergency Management. (2019). Emergency management. Virginia Tech University. Retrieved from emergency.vt.edu.

Virginia Tech Review Panel. (2007). *Mass Shootings at Virginia Tech: Report of the Review Panel* (pp. 1–260) (Commonwealth of Virginia, Governor Tim Kaine). VA: https://governor.virginia.gov/media/3772/fullreport.pdf.

Virginia Tidewater Consortium for Higher Education (VTCHE). (2016). About VTC. Retrieved from http://vtc.odu.edu/about/.

Waugh, Jr., W. L. (2004). Terrorism, homeland security and the national emergency management network. *Public organization review, 3*, 373–385.

Weick, K.E. (1976). Educational organizations as loosely coupled organizations. *Administrative Science Quarterly, 21*(1), 1–19.

Weisburd, D. L., Groff, E., & Yang, S. (2012). *The criminology of place: Street segments and our understanding of the crime problem.* New York, NY: Oxford University Press.

White House. (2021). Executive order on improving the nation's cybersecurity. Retrieved from: https://www.whitehouse.gov/briefing-room/presidential-actions /2021/05/12/executive-order-on-improving-the-nations-cybersecurity/.

Whitman, J. Q. (1998). What is wrong with inflicting shame sanctions? *Yale Law School Legal Scholarship Repository, 107*, 1055–1092.

Williams, T. A., Gruber, D. A., Sutcliffe, K. M., Shepherd, D. A., & Zhao, E. Y. (2017). Organizational response to adversity: Fusing crisis management and resilience research streams. *Academy of Management Annals, 11*(2), p. 733–769.

Wood, D., Konvitz, E., & Ball, K. (2003). The Constant state of emergency? Surveillance after 9/11. In K. Ball & F. Webster (Eds.), *The Intensification of Surveillance: Crime, Terrorism and Warfare in the Information Age* (pp. 137–150). London, U.K.: Pluto Press.

Yin, R. K. (2018). *Case study research and applications: Design and methods.* 6th ed. Thousand Oaks, CA: Sage.

Yin, R. K., & Davis, D. (2007). Adding new dimensions to case study evaluations: The case of evaluating comprehensive reforms. *New Directions for Evaluation, 113*, 75–93.

Zdiarski, E. L., Dunkel, N. W., & Rollo, J. M. (2007). *Campus crisis management.* San Francisco: John Wiley & Son.

Zugazaga, C., Werner, D., Clifford, J. E., Weaver, G. S., & Ware, A. (2016). Increasing personal safety on campus: Implementation of a new personal security system on a university campus. *College student affairs journal, 34* (1), 33–47.

Index

About the Author

Dr. Antonio Passaro, Jr. is department chair and Professor of Criminal Justice at Tidewater Community College, Norfolk Campus, Norfolk, Virginia. Dr. Passaro pursued a career in higher education and leadership following more than sixteen years as a sworn member of the Virginia Department of State Police, attaining the rank of Senior Trooper and, lastly, Special Agent, focusing on High Tech crimes with the department's prestigious Bureau of Criminal Investigation (BCI). He also served with federal law enforcement agencies, Immigration Custom Enforcement (ICE), and NASA.

Among his foremost interests are the examination and study of the underlying and precipitating motivations for criminal and associated deviant behavior on the premises of educational institutions; developing best practices, on a proactive basis, for the prevention and response to these events; and researching, examining, and analyzing existing protocols that address the prevention and response to such incidents.

Dr. Passaro's field experience has provided great clarity and recognition of the fact that, even with the best of plans, the actions required to achieve the intended goal, and sometimes the results themselves, can reflect little similarity to the adopted plan. Accordingly, he has taken into consideration the gaps that often exist between planning and execution, and has researched, examined, and formulated flexible operational safety plans that have application across the broad range of higher educational, commercial, and industrial institutions, to include primary schools through facilities accommodating and meeting the needs of post-secondary education.

The author's highest objective is that his work will further contribute to the Roman orator Cicero's maxim *Salus populi suprema lex*—"The safety of the people is the highest law."

In addition to having been awarded a Doctorate in Higher Education Leadership with emphasis in Criminology and Criminal Justice by Old Dominion

University, Dr. Passaro is a graduate of NASA's Federal Law Enforcement Training Academy at the Kennedy Space Center, numerous other law enforcement training sessions sponsored by state and local law enforcement training academies and agencies, and the FBI-LEEDA Law Enforcement Training Institute Trilogy. He has also been recognized by the Office of the United States Attorney, Eastern District of Virginia, for "outstanding and dedicated public service," and Mothers Against Drunk Driving for his contributions to traffic safety as a sworn member of the Virginia Department of State Police.

Dr. Passaro is a lifelong resident of Virginia Beach, Virginia, who, in his spare time avidly pursues the diverse interests of physical fitness in his home gym; acting; and writing. He has appeared in the Investigation Discovery series, including episodes entitled *Wicked Attractions*, *Ice Cold Killers*, and *A Moment of Clarity*.